Letters to Hannah

WWII recollections of
Hastings & South East England

Written and compiled
by Victoria Seymour

First published in 2003
By Victoria Seymour

Copyright Victoria Seymour.

Email: mail@victoriaseymour.com
Website: www.victoriaseymour.com

ISBN: 0-9543901-1-3

Printed in Great Britain by

impression IT.
26, Brunel Road
St Leonards on Sea,
East Sussex
TN38 9RT
www.impressionit.co.uk

Also by this author;
Letters from Lavender Cottage, Hastings in WWII & Austerity

'Letters to Hannah' is dedicated to my brother, Ron Burkin.

Thanks go to The Hastings and St. Leonards Observer for information and images, to Hastings Museum, Hastings Fishermen's Museum and to the staff of Hastings Reference Library for their services. Also thanks to Colin Allchin for web site construction services, to Adam Allchin and Chris Law for additional photography work, to Ivor White, James Meredith, Helen Edith Stephenson for image contributions and to all those who provided family photographs.

My gratitude to all those who recounted their WWII experiences for this book: Joyce Brewer, Ivor White, David Evans, Marie Gale, DeeDay White, Monica, Noel Care, George Demeza, Christine Demeza, Jean Lack, Rose Brant, Doreen Baldwin, John Bell, Margaret Wilson, Rosemary Oni, Clifford Higham, Mrs Ted Dyke, Dave Harvard, Charles Brazier, Victor Bulger, Bill Gayler, Christine Hayward, Frank Strudwick, Jim Sadler, Bob Gallagher, Ivor Thornely, John Bryant, Bob Champion, Ray Gladwish, John Gill, Francis Cornwall, Norman Redford, Espero, Michele Farman and Joyce and William Hastings.

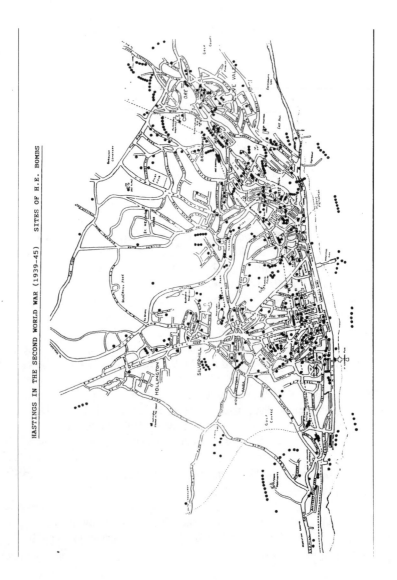

HASTINGS IN THE SECOND WORLD WAR (1939-45)   SITES OF H.E. BOMBS

Dear Hannah,

You were born prematurely in the small hours of a winter morning in 2003. The family waited your arrival with a mixture of joy and anxiety. That night, a power failure had hit my street and the underground cable was being repaired. I sat in chilly, candle-lit gloom, as the emergency repair team worked outside my house. My concern for your mother and you, the clattering of a pneumatic drill and the voices of the workers made sleep impossible. These cold, tense hours brought back memories of nights in my WWII childhood, heightened at that moment by talk of a coming war in Iraq.

Your father, feeling relieved and happy, came to my home at dawn, directly from the hospital; your mother and you were recovering well. He had a photograph of you, newly born and weighing just over two and a half pounds. We scanned the photo and emailed the image round the world, to family and friends.

While your mother, Angelique, was expecting you, she played a significant role in the writing of my first book, based on a collection of WWII letters. She read the transcripts of the letters and asked me so many questions about the history of the times that I decided to use her curiosity as a way to tell the story, in the form of letters addressed to her. The book is called 'Letters from Lavender Cottage' but it could just as easily have been called 'Letters to Angelique'.

After the book was published, I received letters, emails and telephone calls from its readers and a number of the older people told me about their wartime childhoods. Some who recounted their experiences were complete strangers and others were members of your family and my friends. I felt that just as in the case of the Lavender Cottage letters, here were stories that needed to be told.

Before you were born I considered what my role in your life might be, perhaps the 'Story Gran'ma'. So this book, 'Letters to Hannah', is my first story for you.

With very much love, from Gran'ma.

1939

The summer of 1939 had been a poor season for Hastings; the threat of impending war had discouraged many people from taking holidays but on the late August Bank Holiday weekend, perhaps realising it might be a last chance, crowds flocked to the town, which hosted 100,000 visitors. Many residents still refused to believe that war could be a possibility. There were objections to the corporation's plan to remove the seafront illuminations as it would, 'create war-panic, discourage holiday makers and frighten the elderly'. But preparations for war had been apparent for some time; in the week following the August Bank Holiday, Hastings mounted an overnight, civil defence exercise and simulated air raid, to test the emergency services. To keep the public informed, leaflets giving advice for every wartime eventuality and emergency issued forth from government departments. Gardens had been excavated to install Anderson Air Raid Shelters, walls of sandbags were built to protect important buildings and the voluntary services were being assembled and trained. Hastings witnessed the departure of men and women into the military services and the arrival of the first evacuees from London.

A Public Information leaflet was issued that outlined the plans already laid to evacuate millions of children from areas of greatest danger, big cities and towns, to the countryside and coast. The leaflet, designed to allay the fears of families who felt they would rather stick together in the coming times of trouble, assured that, 'the children would be offered homes where they would be made welcome and well looked after'. Mothers could accompany children below school age and provisions were also made for expectant mothers and the blind. The rest of the population was to stay put and contribute something to the war effort, either in a military or civil capacity. Before departure, children carried out rehearsal evacuations, assembling at appointed places, usually schools, with the designated amount of belongings. For the actual departure, coaches and trains were commissioned to transport the children, sometimes to unknown destinations. Parents might not hear of their child's new location for several days, until they received the official post card, supplied to every evacuee. The homing of the newly arrived evacuees was sometimes a distressing process; the bewildered and tired children were lined up, in a village hall or public place, for the not-always-enthusiastic hosts to select them. Farmers looked for sturdy boys, the sentimental wanted pretty girls; few wanted a family group, or the sickly or unattractive children.

These sad little creatures might then be subjected to the exhausting process of being marched round the community, while the evacuation officer knocked on doors, trying to force their charges on to uncooperative households. It is no wonder that some of these children became the victims of abuse or neglect. It seems that there was neither time nor will to match children and hosts socially or according to their religious upbringing. Eventually, a high percentage of evacuees returned to their families; either the sorrow of separation became too much to bear, or the parents were not happy with their children's circumstances, preferring the dangers of air raids to the risk of their children being ill-cared for. It would be unfair to assume that all families who accepted evacuees were unwilling hosts; they too had difficulties. Some of the new arrivals came from slum areas; the children and their mothers might be in poor health and owning only the inadequate clothing they were wearing.

It seems that in general Hastings extended a good welcome to the evacuees. The local paper published a selection of evacuees' observations and remarks, which unfortunately drew a picture of children not used to clean homes and beds, regular meals and frequent bathing. The children's belief that any and all crops were free for the taking led to many misunderstandings. Scores of them had never been outside their city environment and they were full of wonder at the sight of the sea and cliffs. One child, unaccustomed to hills, described Hastings as having "lop-sided roads".

For local children life was also changing and a Hastings girl, Monica, remembers her childhood days as war approached: "The likelihood of war only took on reality for me when we were issued with gas masks. It seems rather an awful thing to say but I couldn't help feeling slightly excited, as we traipsed down to the local community hall to collect ours. Even an outing like this made a change in our austere and frugal childhood. In that same autumn our Dad's business collapsed and this was followed by a breakdown in his health; a very severe winter didn't help things. Then poverty struck the family and for a time the only income we had was the five-shilling dockets, given to us by the Catholic Church. We had a very lean Christmas but we did get quite a kick from a 2/6 (12½ p) postal order, which was sent to us by an aunt. Once it was cashed we would buy each other little 3d (1½ p)gifts from Woolworth and carefully wrap them up. It snowed heavily at Christmas that year and in spite of being hardup I can still remember how lovely it all seemed. We got through these hardships and in the spring Dad acquired a job in Short's aircraft factory, in Maidstone. He took up weekly lodgings there and eventually the whole house became vacant and he took the opportunity to rent it and we joined him. For once there was a bit more cash around and it looked as if we would get some schooling, the Catholic School was actually within walking distance.

In July 1939 we had our very first holiday; for four weeks we stayed with an aunt, just outside the New Forest. The object of the holiday was to prepare and kit us out in preparation for boarding school. My sister and I were to go to the convent our late mother had attended, with my brother going to the college where her brothers had been educated. I enjoyed the holiday but events were to change everything. We had just got home from church, when we heard that never to be forgotten speech by Neville Chamberlain, saying we were at war with Germany. Because of the war Dad wanted us all to remain together, so the boarding school education was never to be. Anderson Shelters were delivered and installed and we were so proud of Dad, as the one he dug out was the deepest and neatest around. Everything seemed to be going a bit better for him job wise until he had a fall at work before Christmas and was off work".

Dear Hannah,

At the end of August 1939, my parents took my two older brothers, Derrick fourteen, Ron twelve with me, aged nearly five, on a visit to Glastonbury, in Somerset, where we all stayed with my mother's friend, Mrs Lillian West. I saw the sea for the first time on a day trip to

Burnham-on-Sea. On the 3rd September we had just returned to our home in Chislehurst, a few miles outside London, when war was declared in an 11.00am radio broadcast, by Neville Chamberlain. The air raid siren went immediately afterwards, a dismal sound that was to haunt the nation for years. It was a false alarm but we did not know that at the time. The younger of my two older brothers Ron, very small for his age, was returning the big suitcase that we had borrowed from our Aunt Kit, who lived in the next street. Ron was terrified on hearing the siren but instead of dumping his burden in somebody's garden he ran all the way back home, with the cumbersome suitcase bouncing against his skinny legs. My father, who had joined the ARP some time before the war, went out on patrol but he put in a duty appearance outside our sitting room window, to check we were wearing our gas masks.

The Burkin children at Burnham on Sea

It was my father's nature to be concerned with 'what's right', as he used to say. This meant that he carried out his ARP duties to the letter. Having been told that no civilians should be walking about after the siren had sounded, he went as far as threatening to thump a cyclist, who would not go in the public air raid shelter because he was anxious to get home to his wife and children during the alert. The man complained about my father to the authorities. With the outbreak of war, some ARP Wardens were compelled by the government to give up their employment, so that they could take on full-time emergency duty. My father was one of these, a move that upset his employer, Mr M, to whom my father was gardener. As the Phoney War set in, it seemed that a permanent emergency force was not needed and, possibly because of his rigorous interpretation of the rules, my father was demobilised. When he went to Mr M, to ask for his job back, he told him to 'clear off'. As the air raids began, it gave my family a grim satisfaction that the house of Mr M was the first in the village to *be destroyed by an enemy bomb; Mr M was away at the time.*

My father had a number of abilities but his calling was as private gardener and jobs in that line decreased, as the rich people evacuated themselves. My mother earned a little money, scrubbing out the Church of the Annunciation and cooking and cleaning for the vicar and his family. It was left to my brother, Ron to look after me when she went to work. Derrick had started work, as was then customary at the age of fourteen; Ron and I could not go to school, as they were all closed, so he became my first teacher. He taught me the alphabet, with the aid of a pack of Lexicon playing cards and set me on the road to learning to read. He also showed me to how to whistle, an accomplishment that I chose to demonstrate to my mother in the church, as she was scrubbing the aisle, bringing down on her and me the disapproval of the ladies of the church flower-arranging group. During the evenings, Ron used to go and help my mother in the vicarage dining room and kitchen, not for pay but so that she could finish earlier. He learned how to lay a formal dinner table correctly, with silver and wine glasses and he helped her wash up. My brother used to look scornful when the vicar's wife called him, 'the little butler'!

We were facing Christmas in poor straits; my father had no full-time work, he was just earning bits of money at odd jobs. Our biggest excitement was the making of a few paper chain decorations, from a packet of glued strips. On Christmas Eve, my mother and Ron went to Midnight Mass and afterwards they walked home in the blackout, knowing that they were going back to nothing. When they got indoors they found a huge basket filled with Christmas goods; a chicken, plum pudding, port wine, tinned goods, chocolate, sweets and other treats. A Mrs Smith, one of the church flower ladies, had won the hamper at a Whist Drive and passed it on to my family. It seemed the whistling was forgiven! After Christmas, my father got a job as a caretaker and gardener in Sutton but there was no accommodation for a family so we stayed in Chislehurst and became one of the many WWII, single-parent families.

With very much love, from Gran'ma.

The Air Raid Precautions Act of 1937 had brought the ARP into force as an organisation. Volunteers began training for all aspects of Air Raid Precautions work, guided by a stream of government handbooks. The Home Office monitored the efficacy of the ARP system during the Munich crisis and learned from it. ARP wardens were the pivots of the local Civil Defence system. They were divided into sectors, each of which had several wardens' posts. These posts occupied a variety of premises; some were set up in ordinary houses but the service gradually acquired purpose-built, reinforced shelters. ARP wardens became the object of public jokes and complaints and were regarded by many as interfering busybodies, even in more dangerous times. The inactivity of the Phoney War gave rise to squabbling in Hastings' Council Chamber about war footing, administrative measures. Questions were raised on who should pay for the premises and the salaried positions of the ARP and what had happened to the 105 citizens who had enrolled for Air Raid Precaution duties and from whom nothing had been heard since?

Even children became involved in the business of preparing their country for enemy attacks. Ivor White, aged 13, was a pupil at Battle and Langton School in September 1939. His early days had been idyllic; he was born in a picturesque estate cottage, in the shadow of Battle Abbey in Sussex and on the brink of the field where the 1066 Battle of Hastings was fought. This spot and its surrounding woods, lakes and slopes were where he and his young friends played and waged their boyhood 'wars'. Ivor recalled the arrival of air raid shelters at his school. "We had been told to bring spades and shovels, so that we could dig holes in the field, beside the boy's playground, to accommodate a number of Anderson Shelters. These were delivered to the school in sections, complete with nuts, bolts and plans and we were also expected

Ivor White aged 13

to construct them. We were bursting with excitement, as we were formed up in the playground to be marched into the field, with shovels 'sloped'. Next to me in the parade was my friend, Michael Poole. We

7

lined up in the field and began; Michael worked opposite me, as we sliced away the turf on our plot. This turned out to be a very bad arrangement. It wasn't long before one of Michael's powerful strokes missed the ground and the edge of his spade hit my left leg. I felt sickening pain and blood was running down my leg. Our teacher, 'Moggy' Morgan, ran into the school for the first aid kit. He did a very professional job of bandaging, or so said my Dad, who was a St John's Ambulance Volunteer. These days it would have been given several stitches and healed without trace but I still have the scar. I am quite proud of my first 'war-wound!'"

The Anderson Shelter was really intended for domestic use. From the end of February 1939, the first Anderson shelters began to be delivered to householders in London and later to other areas. The Anderson shelter was issued free to all earning less than £250 a year and at a charge of £7 for those with higher incomes. These self assembly shelters consisted of fourteen sheets of corrugated iron and when connected they made a living and sleeping space six feet high, four and a half feet wide and six and a half feet long. A trench of the appropriate dimensions was dug, in which to sink the shelter and its exposed roof area was covered with at least fifteen inches of soil.   In 1939, Hastings property agents, Fryer and Sons, were inviting buyers to view their show house at 11, Harold road, where a family air raid shelter was already in place in the back garden. A free air raid shelter was offered to each house purchaser. A local historian claims that one of these Harold Road shelters is still in situ. Another type of public shelter was a one-storey brick and concrete surface-standing building, designed to hold 50. They were cold and dark and had no sanitary facilities. Their poor construction also made them dangerous and deadly places. A nearby bomb burst could lift the roof, usually a concrete slab, which could then come crashing down on the occupants. These defects were later overcome by the building of outer blast walls, the improvement of the mortaring of the cement joints and by edging the roof, so that it could shift a few inches without falling off the supporting walls. There were public underground shelters, which were eventually lined and roofed with either concrete or steel and had closed entrances, initially these also had no sanitary facilities. In common with the Anderson, they were liable to flooding. Some businesses improvised shelters for their staff and members of the public in the basements of strong buildings.

Boys too young for military service were keen to help the war effort; David Evans of Bexhill, aged 15, became a messenger for the ARP and practiced conveying messages by bicycle, from ARP posts in the town to the control HQ. Hastings boy, Noel Care, 15, also volunteered as a messenger and attended a series of lectures about gas, incendiary bombs and the effects of high explosives. He was eventually asked to assist at gas lectures, to hand round phials containing gases for the cadets to sniff and identify. He said, "The scent of geraniums still reminds me of the gas Lewisite, which it closely resembles". With the declaration of war, Noel reported to the ARP Control Centre, where the volunteers did a duty every other night, sleeping as best they could, on settees and camp beds. They passed their waking hours playing cards or draughts and chatting. These night duties ended at 6.30 am. Noel

Noel Care in Red Cross uniform

also became a member of the British Red Cross Society, which introduced to him the first aid skills that would be so vital to his later war work. The nation began to hear the tragic news of the sinking of ships, including HMS Courageous and the Royal Oak. Noel Care's Boy Scout patrol leader, William, had enlisted in the navy in 1938. At the start of the war he was promoted and left his ship, HMS Courageous on 16th September; it was sunk the next day. William then joined the Royal Oak, which was sunk on 14th October; he was aged 20 and the first of Noel's friends to die in the war. After the sinking of the Courageous, William had written to his mother, telling her he thought himself lucky to have been promoted.

On the home front the Food Control Committee started work; suppliers of food stuffs had to register to become licensed or they would not be entitled to trade. On the first day of registration, nearly 1000 licences were granted in Hastings. Customers were to be obliged to buy their groceries from one shop only, for the duration of the war and they had to register with the grocer of their choice. This led to a spate of newspaper adverts in which retailers assured customers of their continuing good service under rationing. Vegetable and fruits were not to be rationed and Hastings green grocer Coopers invested in a series of patriotic advertisements, which were either stirring calls for victory or verses of anti-Hitler doggerel. The butchers protested about the reduction of their meat supplies and thus opened a battle with the food control authorities that would last throughout the war and beyond. Householders came to grips with the new regulations and restrictions that were flung at them. Not the least of which was the blackout. Within a week of war being declared, supplies of blackout fabric were getting scarce. In one day, Mastins, one of Hastings' foremost haberdashers, sold 2,000 yards of black, curtaining sateen, priced at one shilling and sixpence three farthings a yard (7½ p). Also in demand were drawing pins, glue and black paint, as people turned to any means to prevent glimmers of light escaping from their homes and giving an unintentional signal to enemy bombers. Some constructed blinds from slats of wood and black material, carefully measured to fit each window. At night Britain's cities, towns and villages disappeared under a cloak of complete darkness.

By 12th September 1939, the Home Office had opened an enquiry into blackout rules. These became even more stringent and magistrates were seeing cases of infringement as trifling as those caused by the striking of matches or the use of hand-held torches. Serious offenders could be fined up to £100 or given a three-month prison sentence. Hastings saw its first prosecutions for blackout offences in mid-September. The seven in court escaped with relatively modest fines even though, in one case, the light was visible a quarter of a mile away.

The incidence of pedestrian accidents after the inception of the blackout rose dramatically, as people walked into objects or stumbled and fell in the complete darkness. There were 2,000 road accident deaths nationally in the first four months of the blackout, 1,700 more than the average and most of them pedestrians. Torches were subsequently permitted but could have a beam of only one inch in diameter, covered by two layers of tissue paper and always pointed downwards. Pedestrians were advised to wear something white at night, as there were blackout regulations for car headlights. These were concealed behind a louvered metal cover, costing five shillings each (25p). The three louvers were about three inches long and half an inch wide and deflected the light downwards. Motorists were obliged to paint their car bumpers and running boards white. Kerbs and the lower part of roadside tree trunks were also whitened.

In March 1940, a 20mph speed limit for cars was introduced and cycle rear lights became compulsory. Even public transport lights came under blackout rulings. At first, railway carriages were without any lighting but they were eventually fitted with dim, blue bulbs. There was of course, no street illumination but pinpoint lighting was introduced at road junctions. The population was reluctant to venture out into unlit streets and so sought entertainment at home. By October 1939 the sales of radios had increased by 30%. There was a return to creative hobbies and pastimes, as well as playing board games and making music within the family circle.

During September, the Hastings department store, Plummer Roddis (now Debenhams), hosted a recruitment drive for the Women's Land Army, which was open to girls from every walk of life. The WLA was first formed during WWI, in 1917, so that women could replace absent male farm workers and help increase food supplies. The WLA was reformed in June 1939, members were initially volunteers but later conscripts were also recruited; the

1939

Women's Land Army totalled 80,000 by 1944. Recruitment posters picturing happy, healthy WLA girls in rolling countryside concealed the fact that the work was hard and tedious, particularly for those from a non-rural background. Being billeted on remote farms caused isolation and homesickness. More fortunate were those who had accommodation in hostels and many life-long friendships sprang from the shared living and working environment. Long and arduous working hours did not give the girls much time or inclination for a hectic social life and their surroundings offered very little beyond the occasional dance or film show at the village hall. Fortunate indeed were those billeted near a military camp!

The Women's Land Army members certainly looked smart in their dress uniforms of shirts and ties, breeches, short woollen overcoats and neat uniform hats. The work gear was less than attractive and often ill fitting. It consisted of two short sleeved shirts, one green pullover, two pairs of socks, one pair of shoes, one bib and brace overall, one hat, one pair of rubber boots and one long mackintosh of poor quality. From the summer of 1942, members of the WLA had to surrender their clothing coupons. Many farmers were resentful at having inexperienced 'townies' working on their farms, so in addition to learning new and exhausting jobs, the girls had to cope with hostility from the boss and often his wife too! As well as the problems associated with their jobs, health and accommodation, the farming recruits suffered those common to young women; their love lives. A local WLA representative was available to give advice and help but their interventions could be heavy-handed, as they sometimes seemed to forget that the WLA was not a military organisation.

In 1939, the government began to issue gas masks and everyone had to call at the centre nearest to their home to collect a mask and be given a demonstration of how to put it on. These gas masks were issued in a square cardboard box, with a string attached, so that they could be carried over the shoulder, AT ALL TIMES! The civilian respirator had a long, rubber face piece with a transparent eye section. Air came in through a filter in the nozzle, the purpose of which was to eliminate the effects of poisonous gases. The air was expelled via the thin

Civilian gas mask

rubber sides of the face piece, as the wearer exhaled. The whole thing was held on the head by adjustable straps; it made the wearer look both frightening and ridiculous. However, should there have been gas attacks the masks would have undoubtedly saved lives.

There was a specially designed gas mask for children down to about the age of 4 years, but children younger than this presented a problem, as the frequent changes in a young child's developing face made fitting difficult. Therefore, a contoured face piece, which would adapt automatically, was produced, an outlet valve was fitted to ensure good air exchange, to make breathing easier and the filter was smaller. The head harness was fully elasticised and closed with a hook and eye at the back. The design, with a red face piece and blue filter, was meant to lessen the child's fear of wearing the mask and parents were advised to turn wearing it into a game. Its appearance earned the respirator the name of the 'Mickey Mouse' gas mask.

Infant's gas mask

The most unusual respirator was that issued for small babies. The infant was put inside an airtight, helmet shaped chamber, which had a transparent screen; air was pumped in by hand, through filters. It is claimed that most babies fell soundly asleep when placed in these helmets but this may well have been due to oxygen deprivation! The ARP and non-heavy work personnel had a civilian-style duty mask but of a stouter construction. Those who worked in rescue, first aid parties, the fire service and the police had the service respirator, which had the filters in a canvas container attached to the chest, enabling the wearer to work more easily.

Micky Mouse Gas Mask

Dear Hannah,

I have just come into possession of an original WWII gas mask. As I took it from its dusty cardboard box and caught the faint, lingering smell of rubber, memories came flooding back. I put it over my face and at once I recalled my childhood fear of suffocation, as on many occasions, having older brothers helped me, their jokes and antics with this new 'toy' put my fears into perspective. Exhaling vigorously through the mask's outlet valve produced the most wonderful raspberries and this trick, added to our silly appearance, brought me to accept the gas mask and drill sessions. The gas mask's cardboard carrying box has a thin, string cord and I remembered how mine used to cut into my shoulder. My mother's brother, Uncle Mac, was in the upholstery trade and he made us all Rexene gas mask box covers, with proper shoulder straps, which made the box much more comfortable to carry. At the time I had no real idea of the implications of a gas attack or of the

George Demeza on duty at St. Leonards

various forms it could take. I have a copy of the original leaflet issued, advising on what to do in a gas attack, which included how to treat the effects of liquid chemical attacks, using an antidote cream. If the chemical got on your clothes, you were advised to forget about being modest and undress out of doors, a concept that would have shocked my little-girl prudishness!

With very much Love, from Gran'ma.

From the beginning of the war, the Hastings Observer had published photo galleries of local men and women in the services, under the title 'Doing Their Bit'. One of the later galleries featured eight men of the Demeza family, who were engaged on active service; all of them survived the war. Some of the family went to Australia after the war and from there George Demeza sent his recollections of his early service days: "My Territorial camp training was quite tough but I thoroughly enjoyed it. Soon after, when I was aged seventeen, 16 days before war actually broke out, we were mobilized. So we said goodbye to work and family and collected the King's Shilling at Battle. We were billeted over a pub and the first night we went out for a drink. When we got back to our billets the pub was still open and one of my friends introduced me to a drink called Pimms No 1. Next morning I vowed I'd never drink again!

Family On Service

HERE are the five sons and three sons-in-law of Mrs. De Meza, of 63, Canute road, Hastings. Top (left to right): C.M.X. W. De Meza, R.N. aged 22; Gunner P. De Meza, R.A., aged 19; Corpl. George De Meza, O.C.T.U., aged 22; O. S. Ronald De Meza, R.N. aged 18. Below (left to right): B.S.M. James De Meza, S.T.A.C. aged 33; Corpl. N. Spence, Canadian Army, aged 34; Corpl. R. J. Pepper, P.A.I. Force, aged 22; L.C. L. A. Cruttenden, R.A. aged 24.

Source: Hastings & St. Leonards Observer

I don't think I had any thought of what could happen to all those friends and me. I thought it was quite an adventure and treated it as such. Three days later we went to St Leonard's to take up guard duty to defend the beaches and of course, military life started in earnest. At this time, three of our family were called up, Jim, Albert and I. Later there were to be six of us with Bill, Percy and Ron. At one stage there were five of us east of the Suez, with Albert being invalided out.

Still 'posted' at Hastings, I was put on a physical training course. While marching through the big swimming pool we saw a group of young air force boys. There were two of them sparring in a boxing ring and keeping as far away from each other as possible. Unfortunately, it was my nature to think that if you are going to have a fight, you have a fight and I shouted to them to get stuck into it! The boxing instructor stopped my platoon and asked me if I would like to get in the ring with him. I declined, and wasn't I pleased I did, he turned out to be my idol of boxing, British heavy weight champion, Len Harvey! I was also once in a pub at St Leonards, with Joe Louis, the world heavy weight boxing champion, who was in the American air force".

People prepared to try and enjoy Christmas 1939, in spite of the circumstances but on 22nd November, to remind the nation that it was at war and to deter overspending, the government launched the National Saving Scheme, with the patriotic slogan, "Lend to Defend the Right to be Free" The Hastings and St Leonards' shops, though trading with blacked out windows, still carried good stocks of the treats and luxuries associated with the season in peace time. The department stores moved their goods to brightly lit, interior display cases and customers entered the shop via blacked-out, double-door 'light traps'. The government urged householders not to hoard food, other than the usual store cupboard quantity. Little did shoppers realise that it would be many years before they saw the final end of rationing and the return of anything resembling pre-war Christmas abundance.

1940

In January 1940, with the introduction of food rationing, the effects of war began to make their mark even more noticeably on the home front. The first foods rationed were sugar, butter, ham and bacon. The Ministry of Food launched rationing with the slogan, 'Prevent Waste and Protect Ships', pointing out that if merchant ships transported less food then they could bring in essential supplies for the war effort. Rationing was also a system, the Ministry of Food said, 'that would ensure a fair share of food to all of Britain's 44 ½ million people'. The amounts of the newly rationed foods were: bacon or uncooked ham, four ounces, sugar, twelve ounces and four ounces of butter or margarine. (One ounce equals 28.3 grammes). This was per person, per week. Similar restrictions applied to hotel and restaurant portions, where the diners had to be satisfied with one seventh of an ounce of butter and one sixth of an ounce of sugar (two lumps), per meal.

Great Britain suffered the worst winter since 1895. No weather forecasts were published during the war and news items about extreme weather condition were not reported immediately but delayed for 15 days, lest they should be of help to the enemy. That famous indicator of a really hard winter occurred in 1940; the Thames was frozen for eight of its miles, so too were other rivers, docks and, in some parts, the shoreline of the sea. Main roads in Kent were under twelve-foot deep snowdrifts and Hastings experienced heavy snow and 20 degrees of frost. The Dig for Victory campaign was instigated early in 1940 and flowers were to disappear from gardens and lawns and tennis courts were to go from public parks, as every bit of soil was given over to producing crops. Even the South Downs, grazing land for centuries, was ploughed to grow wheat or potatoes.

Monica remembers that in the New Year, her father started to become very ill: "Dad's health was cracking up, an attack of pleurisy kept him from work and he was eventually laid off. We were back in poverty-street and the spring found us on the move to a condemned house, three and a half miles outside Hastings. Even as kids we found the accommodation pretty awful, there were no bathroom or flush toilet and the water came from a well. There was gas lighting, but only downstairs. It was grim but Dad's spirit always seemed to keep us going, we got fun out of picnics when the weather was good. Heaven only knows what we took, probably jam sandwiches with water to drink but we enjoyed it".

Towns where troops were stationed set about doing their best to make their wartime visitors welcome. Some were already billeted in family homes and other Hastings residents were encouraged to entertain the servicemen for a meal or an evening round the fire. During the bitterly cold winter months of 1940 almost 1,000 soldiers made visits to private homes in Hastings and St Leonards. These guests came from Great Britain, Australia, Canada, New Zealand and South Africa. The local Women's Voluntary Service, which had recently moved to more prominent premises in Hastings Town Centre, swung into action and after acquiring the use of St Leonard's Parish Mission Hall they worked at turning the bleak room into a club for servicemen. The WVS plea for furniture, soft furnishings, crockery and a piano brought a generous response and the newspaper photographs of the completed clubroom showed a very comfortable looking set-up.

Dear Hannah,

The Chislehurst schools remained closed for sometime after the outbreak of war; my intended place was at the Church of the Annunciation School. I had recently further disgraced myself again in church, when, not then familiar with traditional hymns, I sang along anyhow, with 'Oh, My Darling Clementine!' and a drunkard's ditty, taught me by my brothers. The song was called 'When the Old Bell Rings'. Possibly my outburst was prompted by the tinkling of the communion service bell! A civilizing influence was clearly needed and I began part-time lessons in a most pleasant way, one that ruined me for conventional school. An elderly, retired head teacher held classes in her kitchen, for a few very young pupils, who were seated at a large, scrubbed table. On chilly mornings, our outdoor clothes were hung near the kitchen range, so that they would be warm to wear home. The atmosphere was cosy and the pace of lessons gentle, with much individual attention and my reading and writing skills blossomed. As I recall it, very little time was given to arithmetic. Later on, the schools re-opened and I had my first experience of a big classroom, crowds of children and a stand-up-and-shout teacher. Our learning progress was tested and when it came to multiplication tables the phrase held no meaning for me. On being asked to write the answer to twelve times three I carefully put down a row of twelve threes! An important part of the day was air raid drill, either as a practice or for a real alert. The school's shelters were of the surface standing, brick variety and even in my childish ignorance I doubted the protection they could provide. During air raids, our teachers would lead the children in singing, to keep up our spirits and to drown out the sound of the guns. How desperate that all sounds now but we were all very young and knew no other kind of life.

With Very Much Love, Gran'ma

Meat rationing, which began on March 11th, was controlled by price-1/10d worth (9p) per week per person, with children under six years old having half a ration. Poultry, offal (liver, kidneys, heart, etc) and sausages remained off ration, as were meals at restaurants. A few weeks later, Lord Woolton, creator of the famous vegetable pie, left the Ministry of Supply to become Food Minister.

In July 1940, Lord Beaverbrook appealed to the women of Britain to surrender their aluminium pots and pans, to make war planes; Spitfires and Hurricanes. Millions of cooking utensils were taken to the special depots

The WVS on scrap collecting duty.

set up by the WVS. When war was declared the WVS had a core membership of 165,000, which came from all sections of the community and also included men. After a short interval and with the changing nature of the duties of the organisation, it became known as the Women's Voluntary Service for Civil Defence. A total of 241 members of the WVS died in WWII, in service to their communities and country.

The WVS was involved in many aspects of evacuee work and assisted in the mustering, care and re-homing of thousands of small children and their mothers. The WVS ran the food centres called British Restaurants, which provided plain but nourishing meals at low prices. Their welfare work for the troops and civil defence services has passed into legend. The WVS mobile canteens appeared at the scene of rescue work after heavy raids, at the points of return of battle-weary servicemen; in fact, in any emergency where a cup of tea and a friendly smile were welcome. In the spring of 1940, thousands of European refugees came to Great Britain and it was the WVS who received, fed and clothed them. The part the WVS played on the home front in WWII cannot be over estimated and the range of their tasks was enormous: They re-housed people who were bombed out, distributed ration books, provided servicemen of all free nations with social clubs, held dances and community events and helped with the family problems of service personnel on compassionate leave. In the wake of air raids they broke the news of death and escorted the bereaved families to mortuaries, to identify loved ones. Salvage collecting was the special mission of the WVS volunteers; they ran salvage drives for metal, paper, glass and rubber. Clothing was collected and placed in special WVS stores; these clothes were used for people who had been bombed out of their homes and had nothing to wear but what they stood up in. When they could, the WVS also helped with providing re-placement furniture and household goods; they also ran a clothes swap scheme for children's wear. Wherever a commodity could be saved or recycled it became the province of the WVS. They ran make do and mend classes, ration-book cookery classes and collected wild rose hips, to be processed into vitamin C syrup, which the WVS volunteers would then hand out to mothers and babies. They organised campaigns for knitting 'Comforts for the Troops' (a slogan that inevitably led to much ribaldry). The WVS promoted a drive to collect millions of books that were distributed to servicemen who were posted to isolated camps. No job was too menial; they wove dusty and dirty waste textiles into camouflage nets and swept up in aircraft factories and sorted the discarded nuts and bolts.

Hotels and guesthouses had great hopes of the 1940 Whitsun Bank Holiday being very successful but the government cancelled the holiday for civil servants and industrial workers, so the banks, business houses and postal services followed suit. 'Vigilant', who wrote a weekly, comment column for the Hastings and St Leonard's Observer, said that the measure, 'would impress Hitler that we are in earnest...there is no holiday for the men who are fighting'. The cancellation of the Whit Holiday seemed unimportant in the face of new emergency legislation, rushed through on May 22nd, which gave the government almost unlimited power over the life, liberty and property of all citizens. On the same day, a Belgian steam tug arrived at the landing stage of Hastings Pier. It was packed with women, children and elderly men, who were, 'sea soaked and haggard'. They carried bundles of belongings that they had snatched from their homes in Belgium, ten days previously. The mate of the tug said that everything that could float was getting out and as they left the port it was going up in flames.

Germany's invasion of Luxembourg, Belgium, Holland and France placed the enemy a mere 22 miles distant, across the channel. Due to newspaper reporting restrictions it was more than two weeks before Hastings was able to read about local men who had escaped in the dramatic evacuation from Dunkirk that had begun at the end of May. One escapee was 21 year-old Trooper Ronald Olley, of The Croft, Hastings. He said that the retreat was an orderly and disciplined retirement, in which they destroyed war materials as they fell back. Of the departure from the Dunkirk beaches he said: "We had no sleep or rest for three days and then we left Dunkirk on a little paddle steamer, I don't remember its name-it was just a pleasure vessel. As soon as we left the harbour we were heavily shelled. The decks were crowded with men, there was no cover but everyone behaved with perfect discipline. We were attacked by a squadron of Messerschmitts, which machine-gunned the decks of the ship with murderous fire. They also fired cannons and used incendiary bullets. There were many casualties, our machine gunner was killed in the first burst of enemy fire but then the

RAF arrived. The steamer, which had been damaged in the attack, lost power and we were taken to Dover by a tug. I was overjoyed to see England".

Seaman James Woodhams, aged 25, of 27, High Street, Battle, made seven trips ashore to rescue men. He had gone out to Dunkirk on Friday, 31st May, on the pleasure boat Brighton Queen. The crew constructed a make-shift jetty, from a line of abandoned vehicles and not a man was lost. The Brighton Queen went back again on Saturday to pick up French troops. James said: "There were bombs falling all around us but none scored a hit. The blast of one knocked me off my feet, then they got us with the second salvo and the Brighton Queen sank quickly. The water was shallow and most of us swam for it and as the masts and part of the funnel were above water we clung to these and after an hour a tug picked us up and took us to England". He added, "I felt little worse for the adventure".

A local, former WWII soldier, who wishes to be unnamed, gave this account of his retreat and escape from Dunkirk: "Being in charge of an anti-aircraft gun mounted on wheels, my job was to walk round on the ground, as the gun was traversed. On this occasion we were retreating from Belgium, towards Dunkirk and firing at German planes, which were attacking us. Suddenly my number two, who was traversing the gun, stopped, looked down at me and said, 'Bombardier, (Corporal in the infantry) stop hitting me on the arse!' I said, 'Why the hell should I be hitting you on the arse?' What had happened was that a German bullet had sliced off a small area of his buttock and he thought that I had been hitting him! We did get to the Dunkirk beaches and while four of us were in a hole in the sand, waiting for a rescue boat, we were machine-gunned and my three pals were killed. I was picked up by a Merchant navy vessel and taken to Dover".

The national press portrayed this retreat as an occasion for defiance and the troops were hailed as heroes. On 31st May, a Daily Express reporter described the arrival of the evacuating troops in Dover: 'There was a touch of glory about these returning men, as I saw some of them tramping along a pier, still in formation, still with their rifles, still with a grin on their oily, bearded faces. Many had not slept or eaten for days and were dressed in ragged clothes, many had wounds, bound up in make-do bandages-a scarf or a handkerchief. Others carried tin hats that were blasted open like cabbages. Their eyes, bloodshot and half closed, still mirrored a fighting spirit that had not been taken away. It was the greatest and most glorious sight I have ever seen'.

The people of Dover raided their own homes for food, sheets and blankets; they handed out cigarettes, cups of tea, and hunks of bread to the near starving men. When their own household supplies were exhausted they sent boys round the streets with barrows, which returned loaded with food and cigarettes. Many of the men came ashore with dogs they had rescued but these had to be destroyed. One soldier carried a doll, which he had found in Belgium street, outside a bombed toyshop: 'For my young daughter', he said. In a period of seven days 338,226 men were evacuated, 68,000 were listed as killed, missing or wounded; 222 naval vessels and 800 civil craft joined in the rescue operation, of which 6 destroyers and 243 other ships were sunk. Churchill called the operation, 'A miracle of deliverance'. In Hastings, there was a sad, landmark event, the first burial in Heroes' Corner, in the borough cemetery. He was Private Harry Victor Henham, aged 19, of Braybrooke Road, who had died of wounds, received on active service with the British European Forces.

On Dunkirk Saturday, 1st June 1940, at St Mary Star of the Sea Catholic Church, in Hastings Old Town, a Miss Katie McCullen was married to a local school master. At that time she was running a home for twelve blind men, all evacuees from East London. The newly-weds took just a weekend honeymoon and the bride recalled their outward bound train stopping at Tonbridge, where she saw that; 'the station was full of Frenchmen, dirty and tired, the remnants of Dunkirk'. She sat in the carriage and cried. Within a month of their marriage, all the blind men Mrs Cookson had been caring for in Hastings were re-evacuated and the staff and children in her husband's school, Hastings Grammar, were moved to the safety of St Albans. The teacher was Tom Cookson and his new bride's full name was Catherine Cookson, who went on to write the books beloved by so many.

After Dunkirk, things changed in Hastings, the air raid shelters came into use, including the St Clements caves on the West Hill. The army engineers had arrived to begin the work of preparing the town for the

1940

Soldiers erecting barbed-wire on Hastings Seafront.
Source: Hastings Museum.

invasion that seemed likely. The promenade was a mass of barbed wire, with some of its curved prominences sandbagged and converted to serve as gun and observation posts. The headquarters of a heavy artillery regiment and guns were set up outside the town and batteries of 12 inch Howitzers were installed at various locations, from Udimore to Hailsham. One member of this regiment was the youthful Spike Milligan. Hastings was made well aware of the possible terrors in store, as army units prepared strong points and the infantry practiced street and house-to-house fighting. Concrete tank traps were built across open spaces and long ditches were dug in fields, to prevent aircraft from landing. In order to confuse invaders, all signposts were removed; this included road signs, railway station platform signs, advertising placards and any other kind of indication of location. The pier was breached, to prevent it being used as a landing stage by the Germans and a curfew was imposed on the Hastings and St Leonards' seafront. This curfew caught Walter Butler, the owner of the Blue Saloon fish and chip shop in Hastings Old Town, in a curious situation. His premises, on the corner of the High Street, had a seafront entrance, which was affected by the curfew and a rear entrance, which was not. Therefore, he was permitted to use his back door in curfew hours but not the front. To adjust this tiresome state of affairs he was issued with a special permit for his front door, signed by the Hastings Borough Chief Constable. This permit, along with relevant photographs, is part of a display in Hastings Fishermen's Museum. The fish and chip shop is still in business under the name The Blue Dolphin.

Summer 1940 brought the war nearer to Monica and her family: "We could clearly hear the guns from the evacuation of Dunkirk. Dad, I remember, was very distressed and one day took himself into Hastings and on his return he told us he had enlisted in his old regiment and was to be taken on as a driving instructor. He had passed the medical; it could not have been a very thorough one, as he was ill again, with

Local evacuees mustering for departure. Source: Hastings Museum

the old pleurisy, even before his army papers came through. By now, war was becoming really evident and air raids on London were a nightly occurrence. Every evening, during the late summer sunset, wave upon wave of enemy bombers filled the sky; that endless engine drone is never to be forgotten. After dark the searchlights would light up the sky and the anti-aircraft guns would try to bring down the planes before they reached London. When the Blitz was raining terror on the City, quite a number of bombs hit our village but at that time there was nothing too disastrous. The village green was the assembly point for the local Air Raid Wardens and among them were some good looking lads, as yet spared the call up. My sister and I used to vie for the best position, to peep from behind the curtain, to get a good view of the lads and stake our claim to which one we fancied. By September 1940, I was obliged to attend the non-Catholic, local village school but that was short lived. Three weeks into the term I went sprawling in the playground and grazed my knee and what had been a simple graze turned into something really nasty, almost life threatening. A severe infection ensued and I became very ill. By now, Dad had been drafted into the army and was sent to Wakefield in Yorkshire but such was the state of his health that no sooner had he arrived he became ill again and he spent the next two months in an army hospital. He was discharged a few days before Christmas but in spite of everything, we enjoyed the festivities immensely".

In July 1940, due to the increased threat of invasion, the government set in train an evacuation scheme for children from the south east coast. It was not compulsory but the Hastings authorities informed parents that after the evacuation there would be no education facilities in the town, except for private schools. The departure from the town of the children and their mothers reduced its population by a third. A Hastings child, Jean Lack, remembers that distressing day: "I was evacuated when I was about seven years old, together with my brother Peter, aged about six and my sister Margaret, about four and a half; we were pupils at St.Paul's Road School. We went from the school with our gas masks, name labels pinned on our chests and carrying grey sacks, which my father had made for us to drag, as we were too small to carry them. It was total confusion, parents, teachers, children, lots of noise and crying. We had never been out of the town before and didn't know where we were going. We went to Hastings Railway Station and I think my mother must have told me to look after the other two, because I wouldn't let go of them, I even went on the train sideways so I didn't have to let go. It was a long day and we were tired and dirty, and very frightened, when we finally arrived in a village called Houghton Conquest, in Bedfordshire. We were taken round the village, where people picked the children they wanted. No one wanted three children. Finally, when there were no more children left, except us, we were separated. My sister went to one family and Peter and I to another. My sister was very unhappy as she was placed with Chapel people who were very religious, and she was a Roman Catholic. She didn't understand what this implied, but they took their prejudices out on her, making her pray for hours for forgiveness. To make matters worse, no efforts were made to maintain contact between the three of us, even though we must have been only a short distance apart. The strangeness of living in that place, with a chemical toilet, in a barn down the road and a water tap up the lane, was difficult to get used to. We only saw our parents twice in about 18 months. Peter and I had an unhappy start with this family, but were later moved to a delightful couple with no children. We kept in touch with them until they died. I am now 70 years old but have never forgotten the day of our evacuation".

Marie Gale, born in Hastings in 1938, was evacuated to Somerset with her mother, who took a job as a live-in housemaid, in return for board and lodging for them both. Marie remembers: "It was a very big house and run like the one in the television series, Upstairs Downstairs. The head cook was a real Tartar and treated us quite badly. The cook's daughter also worked there and they would gang up on my poor mum and keep the best food for themselves, until the house owner found out and changed things. There was a chauffer, gardener and gamekeeper, so you can see, I was somewhat privileged. On rare occasions, the chauffer would drive me into Weston Super Mare. On one visit there, I had my photo taken, standing on a chair and wearing some dungarees my mother had made me, so that I would look like my aunt, who worked in munitions".

Rose Brant (front right) with her
wartime foster family

Another evacuee was Rose Brant, Hastings resident for the past 30 years, who lived in London during the war. She said: "I was evacuated to Lanner in Cornwall in 1940, with my two older sisters. On arrival, we three girls were subjected to the miserable ritual of being lined up and 'chosen' by the foster families". Rose's sisters were taken as a pair, leaving her behind and very anxious. Six year-old Rose approached a lady, who had only come along to accompany her mother, who wished to board a boy. Rose pulled at the skirt of the lady, Mrs Dunston, and said: "Please take me". Mr and Mrs Dunston and their four children lived in a two up, two down house and there was really no room for an evacuee but Rose's plea touched the kind-hearted lady. Esther Dunston took Rose home and found her a sleeping place in the middle of the bed, with her two grownup daughters. A curtain divided the bedroom, and behind this slept the son of the house. Rose said. "I was so happy in that family, I suppose I was utterly spoilt but I felt much loved. My new 'mother' then tracked down my sisters, who were billeted elsewhere in the village. The war interrupted our education and we either had no school at all or lessons were given in over-crowded classrooms. I was perfectly content with my new family but my sisters became very homesick. At that time my mother and little brother were with my father, who was in the army and constantly moving around the country". In 1942, Rose and her sisters returned to London and a life of frequent and heavy air raids and, two years later, the flying bombs. Rose's most prominent memories of this period are of taking shelter in the London Underground railway stations. She said: "I will never forget our special spot, Platform 2, Chancery Lane Station; there were metal bunks set up along the platform and my sister Mary and I used to sleep in the middle bunk, which my mother enclosed with ropes to stop us falling out. I found the whole experience very exciting, especially playing with other children. We were not allowed to run about so we invented a guessing game, using the wall maps of the underground. The trains used to come through the station till late at night. We always knew when there was a raid on as people used to flood down, some with just blankets to lay on. I particularly remember the American and Polish soldiers, who were kind to us children". Rose has kept in touch with her wartime foster family all her life. She attended the Golden Wedding party of her late foster parents in 1972 and still writes to and visits the surviving family.

One of the most idyllic destinations for South East evacuees was Wren's Warren School Camp, near Hartfield, in East Sussex. The National Camps Corporation, a non-profit making body, had been set up to found 43 holiday camps for children, some time in the early 1930s but only 16 were actually built; Wren's Warren was one of these. With the outbreak of war and the need for safe, rural accommodation for evacuees, the camp acquired an un-planned for use. It became home to hundreds of children, who could study, play and live in a rural setting, away from bombing and under the care of a permanent staff. Every facility they needed was on site, including a school, laundry, boot repair workshop, a two-ward hospital, and an isolation ward, with a resident Nurse-Matron.

The first children arrived at Wren's Warren in spring 1940; among them was Doreen Baldwin, who was aged 11½ years and her brother, older by two years. They were given a meal in the vast dining room and then allocated to one of the five cabin-style dormitories. Each dormitory held 50 children and two of the camp's ten teachers, who not only took lessons but also supervised the children, round the clock. Doreen says, "I remember them being good teachers. We children led an open air life in the middle of Ashdown Forest, where we played and

Wren's Warren girls stir the Christmas pudding.
Source:Unknown

climbed trees, almost unaware of the war until the siren sounded for us to run to the shelters, which were long trenches, covered with sheets of corrugated iron. My friend and I took long walks in the surroundings, now termed, 'Winnie the Pooh Country'. One day, feeling thirsty, we asked for a drink of water from a lady, who was looking over a garden gate. She took us into her house and we discovered from her that she was the wife of A.A. Milne, who wrote Winnie the Pooh. We told her that our teacher read us these stories every bedtime. We sometimes used to walk to the famous bridge and play 'Pooh Sticks'. Once a month, Warren's Wren held a parent's day. They arrived by coach, with loads of sweets and we children put on concerts, plays and gymnastic displays. When my brother was 14 he had to leave Wren's Warren but the teachers, who had become very fond of him, got him a job in the village of Hartfield, with a tea company, which had been evacuated from London. He slept in a lovely property called Hartfield House. When I was thirteen, much to my dismay, I won the scholarship and had to leave Warren's Wren and go home to attend the Fort Pit Technical School. Being at camp taught me how to make friends and get on with people. It made a deep impression on my life and I am grateful for the experience and to our marvellous teachers".

John Bell, a former Wren's Warren boy, has written a booklet of reminiscences of his life at the camp. He recalls the evacuees' daily life in vivid detail; friends and teachers, sports, picnics, gardening and indoor and outdoor pastimes. He writes of walks through the woods to the neighbouring towns of East Grinstead, Forest Row and Crowborough. The evacuees watched the Battle of Britain in the skies above their camp and they saw the Home Guard and soldiers in training in the nearby woods and heath, which on one occasion brought about a tragic accident. John writes, "The accident happened in the summer of 1940, Canadian soldiers arrived just outside the boundary of Wren's Warren and set up a field camp in pine trees. They must have had more on their minds than the antics of a bunch of evacuees and the

Wren's Warren boys tackle the garden. Source:Unknown

vigilance of their ordnance was not all it should have been. After the military exercise, a gang of camp boys found an anti-tank mine. The day after throwing the mine in a stream, three boys went back, retrieved it and used a penknife to prise out the fuse, which exploded. One boy died of his injuries five months later, another was maimed and the third spent nine months recovering in hospital. The Canadians expressed their sorrow and made what reparations they could".

Doreen Baldwin, John Bell and 82 members of the Wrens' Warren Reunion Group returned to the camp for a reunion in 2000, at the invitation of Millwood Designer Homes, who had decided to research the wartime history of the site, before redeveloping it. It was a nostalgic day for the one-time evacuees, as they wandered round the buildings and grounds, re-living 60 year-old memories. Doreen said, "There was a touching reminder of what the whole area signifies. In the Millwood show home there is a coloured glass window on the first landing. It depicts a blue balloon, flying on a white cloud, which goes to show that Winnie the Pooh still reigns at Wren's Warren".

Margaret Wilson, a wartime resident of Hastings, now living in Australia, remembers; "When mum was pregnant with my elder sister in 1940, the nursing home in Hastings was closed because the district nurses had been called up for war duty. So our mum was evacuated with several other expectant mums, to Stratford on Avon. A bus picked them up and during the journey, the bus driver heard a plane approaching and pulled into a lay-by. It was an enemy plane and luckily for them, the pilot did not start firing his machineguns until just after he passed over. By the time the passengers arrived at Stratford, the nursing home had already taken in other people, so the bus driver had to go onto Leamington Spa, where mum stayed until my sister was born. One day, my father was out on the Romney marshes, up a telegraph pole with his mate, doing repairs, when they heard a plane approaching quite low, with guns blazing. It was a Messchersmitt. They quickly released their safety harnesses and dropped into a roadside ditch. Needless to say, he was very dirty when he got home and mum said to him, 'What have you been doing?' He said, 'At least I'm in one piece, we got fired on when we were up a telegraph pole'. Margaret added this intriguing little story; "At one time Mum had to attend the Royal East Sussex Hospital, in Hastings, to have a wart burnt off her hand and there was a rumour going around the hospital that two German brothers, who were working at the hospital as surgeons, were suspected of being spies. When police went to arrest them, they had been taken by car to the top of Fairlight Cliffs and were flown to France in a light aircraft".

Dear Hannah,

Margaret Wilson's reference to German spies sounded like a plot of the WWII detective television series, 'Foyle's War', set and filmed in Hastings; I enjoyed it immensely. As I write, only four episodes have been shown but it already has a considerable following, both at home and abroad. Its star, Michael Kitchen, who plays the lead character Inspector Foyle, has emerged as an unexpected, mature sex symbol and has accumulated quite a fan base, (count me in). I understand from a Foyle's fan website message board that visitors have recently come to Hastings, solely to seek out the filming locations and to be photographed outside Inspector Foyle's 'home', in the Old Town's Croft Road. I saw some of the filming for the series in early

Inspector Foyle's Hastings 'house'.
Source: James Meredith

1940

WWII propaganda, with Hastings' net huts as a backdrop. Source: Fishermen's Museum

summer 2002, including a very short sequence, when a girl in WAAF uniform crossed the road to go to the door of the said house. Real-life Hastings fishermen and boats were used in the Dunkirk episode. I must add that the plot was fictional and none of those rescued from Dunkirk actually came directly to Hastings. In the Hastings' wartime newspaper there were never stories of espionage like those in 'Foyle's War' but censorship would have stopped any being reported. The photograph of the GI, the girl and Hastings net shops is an example of some WWII propaganda and as soon as I saw it, my imagination took over. I wondered if that could possibly be 'Inspector Foyle' standing by the car in the background! By the time you are old enough to enjoy Foyle's War I imagine it will have become a classic, as has Inspector Morse. For Hastings' sake, I hope so.

With Very Much Love From Gran'ma

Hastings and St Leonards was in dire need of ARP members and in a public-spirited move, Plummer Roddis gave up its front-page, summer sale advertisement to make way for a dramatic appeal for volunteers who were, 'Urgently needed at once, to augment the understaffed service, if the town is to be properly safeguarded'. The first air raid

Hastings Town Centre Cricket Ground. Source: Richard H Maynard

on Hastings was on Friday, 26th July 1940 at 7.15am. Noel Care, who had just finished his night duty at the control post, was on his way home and thence to work. He saw that bombs had fallen on the cricket ground (the cricket ground was marked as a harbour on the archaic maps the Germans used) and other bombs had fallen in a straight line from Gladstone Terrace, Whitefriar's Road to Bembrook Road; some classrooms of the Hastings Central School were also damaged. Noel was immediately given the task of delivering messages to various ARP leaders and so arrived late for work, where he was reprimanded for not being on time.

That morning was Noel's first experience of the smell of a bombed building; a mixture of old plaster and wallpaper, splintered wood and brick dust, a smell that was to become all too familiar. In this raid one person was killed, two seriously wounded and seven slightly wounded. Noel said, "At that time, shock was not considered to be a medical emergency, so its victims were not treated nor recorded". Those who were bombed out found shelter in a nearby church and neighbours provided tea and food; a kindness that soon became an established routine. Noel Care began to consider what service he would join. He had planned to go into the Royal Army Medical Corp but a physical disability meant that he would serve on the home front for the duration of the war.

On 24th August, The Hastings and St Leonards Observer launched a shilling (5p) fund, to raise 100,000 shillings (£5,000) to buy a Spitfire. Alderman Blackman pledged £1,000 if the town would raise the additional £4,000. There were hundreds of individual, one-shilling donations made to the newspaper and locals organised fund raising events; whist drives, dances, concerts, even a budgie show in somebody's house. In early September, a crashed Heinkel aircraft and German Air Force equipment was put on public display at Summerfields, to raise money for the Spitfire fund. Ivor White, then aged 14, had just started work and he witnessed the moving of the German plane to its exhibition point. "On my way to work at a farm near Powdermills, in Battle, I saw an RAF transporter, with a Heinkel on it, which was wedged between the banks of the road we called Leg of Mutton Hill. The driver had misjudged the wingspan of the aircraft and although the outer parts of the wings had been removed, the load was still too wide to pass through the cutting. I managed to climb inside the plane's cockpit, while the lads were digging it out. Such was my boyhood enthusiasm for war souvenirs, had there been any unattached bits and pieces in the cockpit they would have joined my collection". Bob Champion, another Battle youngster and clearly luckier in the souvenir hunt, wrote his own experience of the same incident. "When I was eleven or twelve, the RAF was moving a German Heinkel bomber that had been forced to pancake land in a field near where I lived. It was travelling by road on a low loader, and of course was being trailed by

"NEVER WAS SO MUCH OWED BY SO MANY TO SO FEW"

quite a few of the local lads, when the wing got stuck between high banks at either side of the road. Within minutes the plane was swarming with boys and a few girls, all of them hunting for souvenirs, with the RAF men looking on helplessly. I managed to free a gauge of some sort from the instrument panel and ran off with it. I never did find out how they managed to get the plane free, or what happened to it. Unfortunately, my trophy got mislaid, during house moving operations a few years later". By 21st September, the £5,000 Spitfire campaign goal was exceeded by £1,000 and the surplus was put into a fund for victims of air raids. The Spitfire was named Hastings

Noel Care, along with millions of others, watched the Battle of Britain,

The Bombed Plaza Cinema. Source: HSLO

being fought in the skies above England. He saw the RAF fighters repeatedly attack the large formations of German bombers, as they flew across the Channel with their fighter escort. At a height that rendered the aircraft to the size of black dots, the battle would be engaged, to the faint, distant chatter of machine guns and accompanied by wispy vapour trails, while empty shell cases clattered down on the streets and houses. At times, the Hastings lifeboat put to sea to rescue British and enemy crew. Joyce Brewer's youthful impression of the Battle of Britain was that it brought a very exciting time to local youngsters. She said "When the German planes flew over; we watched the aerial dog fights and cheered like mad when a German plane was shot down but it began to get really dangerous. When the bombs began to fall, it wasn't a game anymore and I was frightened".

On 7th September, the town centre department stores, including Plummer Roddis, announced that customers could take shelter in their basement departments and cellars, during air raids. It was this arrangement that saved lives during the shocking daylight air raid in Hastings, on 30th September 1940, the aftermath of which Noel Care witnessed. He said: "I was a grocery assistant in a small store that used to stand close to the Central Post Office in Cambridge Road. Sent on a delivery at 10.25am, I stopped to exchange a few words with Mr Heppell, the Manager of The Plaza Cinema (Now Yates Wine Bar) in the town centre. A few moments after I had walked round the corner and into Queen's Road, a bomb hit the coping of the cinema and exploded in mid air.

I ran back to find a horrific scene of death, injury and destruction. Plate glass shop fronts, including those of Plummer Roddis, had shattered and shards of flying glass and the effects of bomb blast had inflicted terrible injuries on pedestrians in the vicinity of the explosion. Eight people were killed immediately, with the final number of dead rising to 14, many of whom had been terribly mutilated. There were twelve seriously injured and 23 slightly injured. On the ground, outside the Plaza Cinema, were the remains of its manager, covered with a blanket. When I later returned to the grocery shop I found that its window had been blown in and the wall behind it was pierced by dozens of splinters of glass. Had I not gone on the errand, I would have been standing in front of that window, following my morning

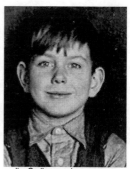

Jim Sadler, aged seven years

routine of weighing up sugar rations". A man who sustained mortal injuries in this bombing was William G. Sadler, aged 39, the Chef at the Albany Hotel. He was on his way to buy some catering supplies and stopped to chat with someone outside a tobacconist shop, which used to be on the corner of Cambridge Road. Mr Sadler died three days later, leaving a widow and four children, the youngest of whom was Jim, aged 2. Over sixty years on, Jim has been traumatized by grief-ridden nightmares and painful feelings of loss for a father he never knew. Jim said: "The war had already separated my family, when the three older children were evacuated. After my father's sudden and terrible death, my mother had a nervous breakdown, so I was cared for by relatives. I have no memory of a proper family life or of playing with my two brothers and sister; it was as if I was an only child". In 2002, Jim Sadler began a quest, to gather some information about his father, a task made more difficult now that so many of his contemporaries are no longer alive. There are many WWII 'children' like Jim, still trying to piece together lost childhoods and family memories.

Dear Hannah,

When the war began, we were renting a ground floor flat in Tudor Court but the rent was beyond the family means. A local man, who had joined the Army, was looking for a tenant for his three-bed roomed semi, for the duration of the war. The rent would be low because the tenants could use only some of the rooms, as the others contained the owner's stacked-up furniture. We moved into these cramped quarters in Woodside Avenue and struck up an acquaintance with the nearby Mitchell family. Mr Mitchell was a policeman and, as was then the custom with policemen, he tended to avoid close friendships with neighbours. But in spite of this, as the night raids began, Mr Mitchell invited us to share his large family's overcrowded Anderson Shelter, as our house did not have one.

Chislehurst is about 15 miles from London's Dockland and for many nights the whole sky was filled with a red glow, as, under a merciless onslaught of bombing, the docks went up in flames. My family waited inside the house one night for a lull in the bombing, before rushing along the back alleyway to the Mitchell's shelter. My father started to run with me in his arms and my mother was halfway down the garden path, being led by Ron, when a mobile Bofors gun opened fire in the road, just outside our house. My mother was transfixed with a terror that increased, as shrapnel rained down, one large

Hannah's Great-grandmother, Violet Burkin

piece hitting the dustbin. It was left to Ron to drag my screaming and hysterical mother to the shelter. Mr Mitchell said the arrangement of sharing the Anderson Shelter could not continue and we would have to go to the public shelter in the Belmont recreation ground. It was too far to run in an emergency, so every evening, Ron pushed a wooden barrow, loaded with blankets and chattels, for our nights spent underground.

My parents had a volatile marriage and at times, to my childish perception, the war seemed just a sideshow to the constant domestic battles. My mother was a lively and attractive London girl called Violet, only four feet ten inches tall and looking far younger than her age. No wonder that my father, six years her junior, fell in love with her, when he first saw her walking in the country lanes of Cudham, off-duty from her housemaid's job at Downe House. Her dainty appearance concealed a determined nature. She had taken a keen interest in the Women's Suffrage Movement and I am told she was adamant about going to the polling station to cast her first vote in a General Election, as soon as she was eligible. She was also an admirer of Marie Stopes, the social reformer, who argued that marriage should be an equal partnership between husband and wife. My father was a very old-fashioned man, who regarded women as inferior to men, in every way. He loved my mother very much but his tendency to be quick to anger and her firm resolve to support her liberationist attitudes meant constant clashes in the home.

I saw the Battle of Britain from the garden of the house in Woodside Avenue. I recall one hot September afternoon, standing on the compost heap, watching tiny planes circle and dive, fighting and killing, against a cloudless blue sky, too high for sound to be audible. Feeling something soft beneath my feet I looked down and saw I was standing in a nest of fat, white maggots, some crawling over my feet. To my child's mind this horrid sight became a part of the picture of death and destruction above me. We continued with our nightly trek to the public air raid shelter, never quite sure what we would see as we emerged. One morning, we found the house backing on to ours had a huge hole in its front garden, caused by an unexploded land mine. The crater was cordoned off but this did not stop a small group of boys gathering round the spot, including Ron, until an ARP warden finally chased them off. Shrapnel and souvenir collecting was the boys' wartime hobby, one which I viewed suspiciously. To me there was something sinister about these jagged, gleaming chunks of quickly rusting metal; according to little girl's gossip, shrapnel was covered in germs. We had never heard the word biological warfare but the similarity of the words German and germ made us come to this conclusion!

With Very Much Love Gran'ma.

Joyce Brewer and her family were evacuated to Wells in Somerset, on 13th September 1940; she loved the peace there. By then she was fourteen; her school days were over so she got a job in the fish and chip shop, above which she was billeted. Wells was crowded with London's East End evacuees, who used to descend on the chip shop every day for their dinners. For Joyce it was a happy and busy time. She settled well in Somerset but the rest of her family felt unwelcome in their billets. Her Mum was sad at being parted from her husband and missed her own home and daily routine. Mr Brewer was a train driver and thus doing work of national importance but his wife hated the idea of him being alone in Hastings. She wrote to her husband and asked him to send her train tickets and the family returned to Hastings, to find it a changed town. Joyce said, "We used to stand on the West Hill Cliffs and watch passing naval convoys in the channel, being bombed by German planes. Because so many people had left the town there were few neighbours remaining for company and there was always the threat of us being bombed". The family had been back only five days when a German aircraft dropped several bombs close by Joyce's home, which was a few hundred yards from a power station and a railway station, both prime targets for the enemy. When Joyce's Dad was away, her Mum turned to her for moral support and to warn her when danger was imminent, so that they could shelter under the kitchen table. Almost every day, the southeast coastal towns had to endure tip-and-run raids. Joyce grew to dread the days when low cloud gave the planes a chance to sneak in and bomb and machine-gun all parts of the town, even before the sirens had sounded; everyone lived on their nerves. There were too few Spitfire and Hurricane planes to attack the enemy and in the early part of the war, there were not enough anti-aircraft guns to spare for the defence of small, unimportant seaside towns.

1940

Joyce said, "The nights were worse. When the London Blitz was on, our house shook, as huge formations of planes passed overhead. I used to lie in bed, with nerves on edge and ears tuned for the distinctive, unsynchronised drone of the engines

The ruins of the Bedford Pub. Source: HSLO

of approaching German aeroplanes. The complete blackout seemed to make it worse, magnifying every sound. There was always the risk that some planes might jettison their bombs over Hastings, to escape from the night-fighters. On really bad nights I could see gunfire flashes and the red glow, from the buildings on fire in London. During the latter part of 1940, my family's only solace was the wireless but even that small pleasure was ruined, when the electric power was reduced, as always happened when an air raid was expected".

For Noel Care, the memories of autumn of 1940 have converged into one impression of continuing air raids. He was not then qualified to administer first aid but he witnessed shocking scenes that have stayed in his mind all his life. His most abiding memory is of the courage of the rescuers and the stoicism of the people of Hastings; he said that you seldom saw tears in public. On the 5th October 1940, the Queen's Road area was the target for 12 bombs, one of which destroyed the Bedford Public House; the licensee and his wife were dug out alive. A street trader, Amos Prior, who sold vegetables outside the pub, was killed. The trolley bus wires were brought down and live wires were sparking and bouncing about all over the road. Five days later, bombs were dropped on the Broomgrove Steel Housing Estate (Tin Town). Noel said of this raid, "On arriving at the scene I was informed by a frightened lady that there was a hole in one wall of her house and something sticking in another. She claimed that the object had whizzed past her as she sat in an armchair. Investigation of other properties

40

revealed a series of similar holes, where a piece of bomb casing had passed through seven walls, before becoming embedded". This housing estate, like Joyce's home, was situated close to the power and railway station. On 12th October, German fighter-bombers dropped 11 high explosive bombs, again in Queen's Road, damaging gasholders, which were sited where the Safeway supermarket now stands. The gasholders burst into flames, throwing out choking fumes and burning particles over the surrounding houses. ARP wardens tried to get householders to close their windows, to prevent the contents of rooms from catching fire and to lessen the risk of breathing problems. Some householders were more concerned that if the gasholders exploded, their windows would be blown in, so they fell to arguing with the wardens about the safest option; they eventually responded to the ARP wardens' forceful language. Thanks to the efforts of a local hero, the fire service and the gasworks staff, the flames from the gasholders were eventually extinguished. The hero was Reginald Grant, aged 26, a Hastings railway motor fitter. He helped to get hosepipes into position and then climbed onto the damaged gasholder, from which flames were pouring through a gash in the metal. He worked for half an hour, filling the hole with clay. In spite of the water from hoses being directed on him he said, " I got pretty well singed" This unassuming man was surprised to be awarded the George Medal and it had not occurred to him that he would be able to put GM after his name. The directors of the Gas Company presented Mr Grant with a cheque

Bexhill boy David Evans and his school had been evacuated to St. Albans, in May, right in the middle of School Certificate Exams. In October 1940, David and his friend decided to cycle home to Bexhill from St. Albans. They left very early in the morning and passed near Croydon, around midday. An air raid was in progress and they saw

David Evans in the Home Guard

the explosions from the bombs and were saddened to see a Spitfire, with one wing missing, spiralling to earth.

They reached Bexhill by dark, and as it was a defended area, with restricted entry, they made their way through the High Woods at the north of the town and eventually reached home. David's father would only let him remain at home if he got a job, so he went to Lloyds Bank in Devonshire Road and asked if he could be of any use to them; he

HOME GUARD

"C" Company—54th Kent Battalion.

(Your own Local Defence Force)

Recruits are Wanted

WHY?

Because so many men of this Company have been called up, or have joined H.M. Regular Forces.

Because more men are needed to take their places and to defend, on a properly organised basis, YOUR Homes in CHISLEHURST District.

The chances of attempted
Invasion have not diminished.

We are giving up a great deal of our spare time preparing to SMASH GERMANS IN CHISLEHURST.

Are you going to leave it all to us?

You'll be no good if and when the time comes unless you are with us, or some other Official Defence Unit.

THINK IT OVER!

And YOU are wanted now!

Age limits—17 65 years.

Apply at "C" Company Right-half H.Q. on the old Conservative Club premises at the corner of Green Lane and Belmont Lane, West Chislehurst.

Any evening, but especially this week 20th-24th October, between 8-p.m. and 10-p.m.

The Otanick Press & Signs, Ltd. Lewisham S.E.13

was taken on as a junior clerk.

By this time, Bexhill was a fortress town. Steel structures had been erected in the sea close to the shore; coils of barbed wire covered the beaches and the promenade end to end, which also had concrete tank traps on it. Windows of many sea front properties were sandbagged, to form machine gun posts and there was a coastal battery of 6-inch guns, hidden within the high promenade at the end of Sea Road. Anti-aircraft pits were dug at intervals along the promenade, to house Bren guns. Concrete pillboxes were erected at vital junctions to give good fields of fire. David decided to join the Home Guard. This organisation, originally named the Local Defence Volunteers (LDV), was established in May 1940. In the Hastings area over 800 men came forward to volunteer for the new force, some arriving to sign up before the radio broadcast appeal for volunteers had finished. In August, the LDV was given the title the Home Guard by Winston Churchill. In the initial period, over a million men & women enrolled in the H G. The hope was that they could delay an enemy invasion force temporarily, to give the regular army time to form a front line from which to repel the invaders. When they were first formed, the Home Guard were expected to fight using nothing more formidable than shotguns, air rifles, old hunting rifles, bayonets, knives and pieces of gas pipe with knives or bayonets welded on the end. The Home Guard was eventually issued with more conventional armaments; mostly remainders from WWI, and later, those sent from America or Canada.

Dear Hannah,

Do not take the television programme, 'Dad's Army' as your model for the Home Guard. Many of the men who joined the HG were WWI Veterans and the military training they had been given years before remained clearly in their minds. Thousands of them were also rural men, already used to handling firearms when hunting game. This had taught them how to move about silently and unobserved. My father, born into a Kent, fruit farming family in 1900, was in the Chislehurst Home Guard from the start; they had their headquarters in a large house on the edge of Pett's Wood, between Orpington and Chislehurst. One night my father's company were sent out on manoeuvres. The company was divided into two, one half to attack the HQ and the other to defend it. The C.O. of the defending section was WWI veteran, Mr Cox, the Chislehurst Common keeper. He was a burly, red-faced man and the village lads, including my brothers, were the bane of his life. Mr Cox and his section stayed awake all night and were pleased that they had been

Chislehurst HG down a Dornier

given no cause to defend the HQ, only to find that the 'enemy' had gained access to the building under the cover of darkness and had spent most of the night asleep in the upstairs bedrooms! The Chislehurst Home Guards were trained by the Sergeant Major of a regiment of Scots Guards, which was billeted in one of the big houses, requisitioned when their owners fled to safer areas. The Home Guards, with full kit and weapons, were trained on the same assault course as the Scots Guards. My father was manning a Smith gun, a piece of small artillery equipment that was usually towed. He stood by the assault course with three others, having a joke, as their comrades struggled with the challenge. The Sgt. Major was not amused and said: 'What do you lot think you are laughing at? That Smith gun breaks down into four pieces, doesn't it? If you think it's so funny then break that gun down and get it and yourselves and it over the course!' That was how my father got the rupture that troubled him for the rest of his days. My father had been a WWI Lewis Gunner and was posted to Cologne during the post war occupation of Germany. In the late summer of 1940, his Home Guard Company was given a lecture on the Lewis Gun, by a Scots Guard instructor, along with a demonstration of how to strip and reassemble it. Noticing my father engaged in conversation during the lecture, the Scots Guard called him to the front, to carry out the procedure just demonstrated. This he did, with perfect accuracy and in double quick time. His reward was to be called a clever dick by the instructor.

1940

The Scots Guards left the village and were replaced by the Grenadier Guards. Their Sgt. Major used to ride round the village on a bike, with his swagger stick under his arm, looking for Guardsmen who were not dressed or behaving according to regimental regulations. I remember my father bringing home his HG kit and weapons, as all members were obliged to do. He had a Lee Enfield 303, ammunition and bayonet and he spent ages cleaning the gun, under my fascinated gaze. In his highly polished boots and freshly pressed uniform he was the re-creation of his younger self, when in the King's Royal Rifle Regiment, in WWI. I thought that he looked like a real soldier and we would be safe from the Germans with him in the house!

To see the HG as just a laughable bunch of old men and boys is a mistake, as this report from a wartime edition of the London Evening news shows. My father was on duty with 19 other HG when a German bomber flew over Chislehurst Common one Sunday in summer 1940. The report ran: 'A German Dornier was machine gunning near a HG gun emplacement and their plane was flying very low, at about 400 feet but the pilot could not see the concealed Home Guards. At their Commander's order, '500 yards-6 yards in advance-rapid fire', the whole Home Guard squad opened fire, some muttering, 'Got him, got him', even before they saw the smoke issuing from the plane's tail. In less than ten seconds, 180 rounds had hit the bomber, which crashed, with all of its crew of five dead, a mile or two further on. Those Home Guards were a mixture of the same you would find in almost any unit of the Home Guards; clerks, shopkeepers, foresters, golf caddies, lads of seventeen and ex-soldiers. The newspaper called them, 'The first Home Guard Detachment to win its spurs in the Battle'. Some were inclined to scoff at the likelihood of this story, of course the newspaper picture is posed, how could it be otherwise? No 'embedded' journalists were covering events on Chislehurst Common! But, knowing my father's pre-occupation with 'what's right' I choose to believe it.

Much Love From Gran'ma

David Evan's Bexhill Home Guards Company paraded for duty every fifth night, at the Drill Hall, where the Company Commander, (David's dentist) detailed off the Home Guards to man various posts around the town and to look out for parachutists and fifth columnists. They carried out sentry duty in pairs, for stints of 2 hours on and 4 hours off. David Evans said, "Trying to sleep on the dirty straw mattresses on off-duty periods was a fitful experience. Occasionally, a returning sentry, discharging the rounds from his rifle, would forget the 'one up the spout' and fire it into the roof. Real Dad's Army stuff"

The Bexhill Home Guards 'action station' was on the north side of and overlooking Pebsham airfield, to the east side of the town. In the event of invasion, David's section would man a sandbagged machine gun post, dug into the top of a small bluff above the airfield, which was covered in poles and other obstacles, to prevent enemy landings. The section leader was aged 17 and apart from David and his friend Hugh, there were about three to four others, mostly young. The Bexhill Home Guard had a water-cooled, heavy Browning machine gun; a gas operated light automatic machine gun and several First World War rifles between them. David said, "No pitchforks or pikes for we front line Bexhillians! They would come off duty at 6.00am, with just enough time to get home, have a wash and breakfast, before reporting for a full day's work. David recalls, "On one occasion, I think it was late in November; we were stood to and reported to our machine gun post in some trepidation. We remained there, without any food and after what seemed like 24 hours we were stood down". For their Home Guard service they periodically received a small subsistence sum, which the 'old sweats' proceeded to take off them, playing pontoon.

David said that air raids were still a constant feature of Bexhill life, but most of the action was in the air, the bombing being reserved for targets inland. He remembers the massed formations of aircraft as an amazing sight, which tended to appear at regular intervals throughout the day, until they suddenly died down, when Hitler switched the Luftwaffe to the Eastern Front to attack Russia. After that, Bexhill withstood quite a lot of hit and run raids from pairs of enemy fighter-bombers, sweeping across the town at low level, dropping bombs. Isolated enemy bombers also dropped incendiaries on the town from time to time. One night, David and Hugh used stirrup pumps to put out fires in the roofs of several houses in Holmesdale Road and Sutherland Avenue.

As David reached the age to volunteer for the Armed Forces, he left the Home Guard and Bexhill, so knew little of what happened in the town after that. He volunteered for service in the Royal Air Force in December 1941 and after flying training in the U.S.A. he returned to Britain to fly fighters; he ended his service a Flight Lieutenant. He said, "Sadly, a number of the more senior boys from my school, who were in the war from the start, lost their lives".

Mrs Rosemary Oni remembers living through the heavy raids: "I was born and bred in Hastings and lived here through WWII, in Milward Road, which was bombed five times. On one occasion, after an air raid, rescue workers were digging and searching in the bomb- rubble of some flats. An elderly couple who lived there never seemed to go out together, so the rescuers were convinced at least one of them was buried underneath the ruins. Imagine the delight of the people when

they saw the couple coming along the road, having providentially decided to go together to collect their pensions.

A house that was three doors from us had a direct hit and a woman was killed there. It was amazing in the circumstances that our house sustained so little damage, just broken glass in the back door. The road opposite our house had flames coming out of the ground. I really don't know what caused that. One day my mum was in the garden and an enemy plane flew over, machine gunning as it went. A roof repairer later told my mum our roof was full of bullet holes.

Everyone whose job was not essential was told to evacuate, due to fear of invasion. On the day we should have gone, my dad, who was a furniture porter, had gone out of town with a removal. My mum was not sure of his whereabouts but our grocer, who held a prominent position in the Hastings Home Guard, felt there would be no invasion here, so we stayed put that day and all through the war.

My parents, my aunt and I all lived in a lower flat with no air raid shelter, during raids we just sat in an alcove, under the front doorstep of the flat above. I thank God we all survived unscathed. People came to stay at our home, those who, for various reasons, couldn't be in their own homes. At one time no one was allowed into Hastings from outside unless they had a special reason for coming, such as visiting a relative. I believe they were checked on arrival at the railway station. They were harrowing days but we still managed to have a laugh."

Dear Hannah,

In October 1940, my family decided to move to Somerset and live with Mrs West, my mother's friend. Although it was certainly peaceful in Glastonbury, another move did not help my education or feelings of stability. Mrs West's house was in Beckery Terrace, at the foot of Weary All Hill. Behind the house there ran a murky brown river, home to eels, which my brothers and the village boys used to catch. My father found work, building airfield bunkers for the Ministry of Defence. I attended a little school in Glastonbury and once the children had got over my non-Somerset way of speaking I was eventually accepted as a member of a small gang of children, who happily roamed the countryside, having fun, much as the children do in the lovely book for children, 'Goodnight Mr. Tom'. I have a copy of this I am saving for you, Hannah. You will be surprised how far ahead I am planning your

1940

reading list!

Looking back, I appreciate how wonderful Mrs West was to accept a family of five from London into her little home, which already housed five people, including her demanding, elderly father, known as Gramfs. We stayed in Glastonbury for a year and I loved every season, as it changed the surrounding countryside. In the winter, the frozen water meadows were perfect for skating and sliding and in the summer the hayfields were adrift with a huge variety of wild flowers. These days, pesticides have put paid to such glorious sights. In the autumn, I managed to fall in the rain- swollen river and was rescued by a soldier, on his way to the railway station to go on leave. He was none too pleased to have his uniform drenched!

With Very Much Love Gran'ma

Ivor White remembers his 14th birthday in November 1940: "I volunteered to join the Royal Army Ordnance Corps as an Armourer but after an entrance examination at Preston Barracks, Brighton, I was disappointed to learn that I had failed the algebra test and would have to wait another 12 months to re-apply. That was when I decided to join the Home Guard instead; I could not wait to get into uniform. After coming back from the army exam in Brighton I went to see Mr Clarke, my Headmaster and he agreed to give me algebra lessons after school. I was unable to progress with what then was a 'black art' to me and after a few weeks I gave up and looked forward to joining the Battle Home Guard".

Salvage collecting continued with no let up. Scrapped newspaper was fetching a penny for three pounds and magazines a penny for four pounds, pleasing enterprising small boys. The Ministry of Food urged housewives to cook more potatoes and, as onions were in short supply, to use leeks as a substitute. MOF, pre-Christmas newspaper announcements declared 'Shop patriotically- buy just one half or even one third of your usual requirement of imported dried fruits for Christmas pudding or cakes'.

1941

Noel Care, who became 18 years old on Christmas Day 1940, put in for a transfer to the Civil Defence First Aid Section and reported to their Frederick Road centre in early January 1941. Noel learned advanced first aid and the techniques of rescuing casualties from craters, cellars and wrecked buildings. One of his colleagues owned a house, in Whitefriar's Road, which had been bombed and this site proved to be a valuable training ground. To act as the 'casualty', the services of a Civil Defence trainee, a member of the public or a child were enlisted. The volunteer would be tied to a stretcher, which was then put through a series of hazardous hoisting and lowering manoeuvres. This called for skill in a range of knots. Noel was grateful to his seafaring uncles at Rye, who had taught him to tie knots, when he lived among them as a child.

The Minister of Food, Lord Woolton, pegged British food prices on 14th January to prevent racketeering. Controls were placed on coffee, cocoa, honey, tinned food, meat paste, rice, pasta, pickles, sauces, jellies, custard, biscuits, nuts and processed cheese. Hastings grocer, Arthur Fellows, found himself in court for rationing offences; he had disposed of 50 pounds of butter and 32 pounds of margarine without returning the corresponding coupons to the Food Office. He claimed, in his defence, that his business was in a colossal muddle but he was still fined £13. Later, there came the rationing of all conserves to eight ounces per person per month. Hastings Woolworth store was fined £12 for selling jam for a sum exceeding the controlled price and in improperly labelled jars. The offence was uncovered by the Hastings Food Controls Enforcement Sub-Committee Inspector. He said that the jam, at 11½d (4½ p) per pot, was 28% overpriced and that every penny counted to many people in Hastings.

LET US GO FORWARD TOGETHER

Communal Feeding Centres were established in the town, to provide the public with cheap and nourishing meals. With the evacuation of so many women, children and non-essential residents, family structures had broken down and this feeding scheme ensured that there was a source of at least one hot meal a day available to those managing on their own. These Feeding Centres were set up in unused schools and church halls and staffed by the ladies of the WVS. The public did not like the title, 'Communal Feeding Centre', so the local paper ran a contest for a new name. This brought out the punsters; Cafall-café for all, was one suggestion; another, Plato's, as in 'Pass me your plate-oh'. The winner was National Restaurant, which came close to the final choice of name, the British Restaurant.

By early February, the war was costing the country £11 million per day and the country steeled itself for heavy tax increases. No wonder Winston Churchill saw it as the appropriate time to make a speech to the nation, which ended: 'We shall not fail or falter, we shall not weaken or tire. Neither the sudden shock of battle nor the long drawn trials of vigilance and exertion will wear us down. Give us the tools and we will finish the job'. Churchill's call to the country's patriotism brought a rush of women to the military services that month. Most went into the ATS, the Auxiliary Territorial Service; they were not involved in combat but took on jobs that would free men to fight. The WAAF, Women's Auxiliary Air Force, enjoyed a reflected glory

because of the reputation of the brave Battle of Britain pilots. There was a certain snobbery associated to being accepted in the WRNS, The Women's Royal Navy Service, who worked with the Royal Navy. Because of their strict entry conditions it was assumed that its members were 'ladies'

The Minister of Labour, Ernest Bevin, wanted to, 'Put women in men's shoes', to work in munitions factories. One hundred thousand women were needed for what was unpleasant work, in shell-filling factories. To encourage mothers to work, the government paid half of the shilling per day (5p) child minding fee. A centre was set up in Hastings for men and women to learn how to use manufacturing machinery. Some of the women, who became quite adept at the new skills, declared it was better than housework and looked forward to moving from the role of unpaid, household worker to well paid war worker. Women played a major role on the WWII home front. With husbands at war or away from home on other essential duties, many women found themselves in a virtual single parent situation. As well as bringing up a family on a reduced income and with meagre rations, many undertook voluntary work of all kinds, including that of ARP Wardens. (It was during 1941 that the name ARP was phased out, in favour of Civil Defence). Women also worked in the Civil Defence in every capacity, as telephonists, ambulance drivers, and first aid workers at the scene of bombings. They also took on paid employment in a multitude of clerical and administrative posts, to free men for military duty. They also became bus drivers and conductresses, railway station cleaners and porters.

Monica and her family faced tragedy, when in February their father was taken severely ill with meningitis: "Dad was taken in ambulance to hospital. We did not know we would never see him again. At first he rallied but in March he had a relapse and he died at seven minutes past midnight on 6th March. We thought it was the end of our lives but you have to pick up the pieces. Seven months after my knee injury, the wound had almost healed and at last I returned to school, finding the classrooms very crowded, as they had to accommodate all the over-eleven year-old children together. The curriculum was very limited, just the three Rs and a little history and geography. Quite a lot of the time was spent in singing and country dancing and, being a rural school, we ran a flourishing Young Farmer's Club. A local farmer made a small field available to us, where we caught and killed moles and then cured the skins and sold them, to raise funds. We kept quite number of rabbits and everyone was expected to bring a bag of rabbit food that they had picked on the way to school. We also visited local farms to see activities like sheep rearing in progress".

It was still obligatory to carry gas masks but people were becoming rather blasé about the whole thing, as can be gathered from the comment by 'Vigilant' in The Hastings and St Leonards Observer, on February 22nd. He upbraided his readers: 'Every resident should go through the gas chamber at the Corporation yard at Bo-peep, to test for defects in their gas masks. It is an interesting experience, with no attendant danger'. A mere handful had used this facility. In response to government directives, Hastings Corporation announced that every idle acre in the borough would go under the plough, to grow food crops in the Dig for Victory campaign; the War Agricultural Committee paid for the labour, equipment and seeds. Among sites selected were Harrow Lane football pitch, school fields at Pine Avenue and empty, Hastings Corporation land at Red Lake. Excellent progress had already been made in the 'war nurseries' established by the Hastings Parks and Gardens. There was an unpopular proposal to fill the seafront flowerbeds with beetroot, instead of flowering plants. The eventual profusion of vegetables in allotments, household gardens and easily accessible public places resulted in a spate of crop stealing. Sheep were brought in to graze on the town's Central Cricket Ground and on the East and West Hills, creating a rustic picture of Hastings that had not been seen for a century. Pigs became an important source of British

produced food and householders were asked to put every scrap of waste food in the collecting bins provided. A list of waste items not to be put in the pig bins included the unlikely- glass, tin, soda and disinfectant and the increasingly rare, orange, lemon and banana skins.

Joyce Brewer recalls that in the spring of 1941 the big raids slackened off a bit in Hastings, "But we still had to cope with the fear of tip-and-run raids, though by then the town did have machine guns, sited on some of the higher buildings, which was some comfort but they weren't very effective". Hastings had the arrangements for its bombed-out residents well in hand, with a special scheme to meet emergencies; the loss of housing, furniture, clothing, money and essential documents, such as ration books and identity cards. Hastings was considered to have one of the best, post-air raid rest centre systems in the country. These centres were run for the most part by female volunteers who, in desperate situations, sometimes took the bomb victims into their own homes. Government cash grants for house repairs, travel and compensation for injuries were available. It was advised that people kept an emergency, 'bombed-out kit' at hand, consisting of a change of clothes, overcoat, blanket, cup, soup plate (preferably metal) knife, fork and spoon and a

Hastings St Clements Caves in use as wartime shelters. Source: Hastings Museum.

bottle of drinking water. Schools, closed for some time due to lack of teachers and air raid shelters, remained closed and there were fears for the future literacy of the town. The local authorities were also concerned about public air raid shelters being used for residential purposes. The St Clements Caves on the West Hill already had 200 people sleeping there, with room for more. Classrooms had been set up in the caves for children's lessons and team games were organised on the grassy slopes above.

Joyce's real working life began when she took a job as a Hastings milk delivery girl. Shortage of clothing supplies meant that she had to wear her school uniform at work, as she sat beside the driver, a retired policeman, in an Austin 8 van, while they went round the town making doorstep deliveries. She worked in all weathers, seven days a week, with the daylight, tip and run air raids still going on. One day, Joyce's boss, Mr W E Funnell, got her a pair of hob-nailed boots and these, combined with a second hand, heavy leather coat, provided her with some warmth and protection. Joyce said, "This outfit presented a laughable picture". Milk supplies were not yet rationed but householders were asked to cut back on their purchase of fresh milk by one seventh, to enable stocks to be turned into cheese and tinned milk. Official fire watching groups had been set up at the start of the year and a lecture on the importance of forming fire watching parties at once was given at the White Rock Pavilion, by Alan Wells, the Fire Co-ordinating Officer. The town was divided into sections; each obliged to set up its own fire-watching scheme. Every man on the home front, aged between 16 and 60 years, had to do 48 hours fire-watching duty per month. As it turned out, a huge percentage of the firewatchers were women; the government provided them with training, buckets and stirrup pumps. Sacks of sand to smother incendiary bombs were placed along the street, at the foot of lampposts. These sacks of sand remained in position undisturbed until, as the result of much canine attention, they split, providing heaps of very unhygienic play-stuff to children!

With increased risk to civilians from the bombing raids, Herbert Morrison introduced an indoor shelter. The Morrison Shelter was approximately 6 feet 6 inches long, 4 feet wide and 2 feet 6 inches high and consisted of some 219 parts (not including the 48 nuts and bolts) and came with 3 tools with which to assemble it. These shelters were free to most people and over half a million had been distributed by November 1941. When not in use as a shelter it could be used as a table, by dismantling the wire mesh sides. The Morrison Shelter was very effective, if assembled correctly, and it undoubtedly saved many lives. Great courage was displayed during an early April bombing raid in Hastings, when a local nurse won a George Medal. Miss Dorothy Kate Gardner, aged 23. She was in charge of a private ward at the Royal East Sussex Hospital and while she was trying to get her patients to an air raid shelter, she heard a bomb coming, so she flung herself full length on a female patient to protect her. The hospital received a direct hit and Miss Gardner, who saved the life of her patient, sustained very severe head injuries that incapacitated her for a year. To test the public's preparedness, mock gas attacks were mounted and tear

Mock gas attack. Source: Hastings Museum

gas cylinders were dropped at Hastings' Wellington Place and the seaward end of Queens Road. Luckily for those who had come out without their gas masks, a high wind dispersed the clouds of gas quickly. The nearby town of Battle had previously put on a more dramatic and successful fire alert and gas attack exercise. The Newberry jam factory was chosen as the scene for a tear gas attack and a fake fire. Clouds of black smoke enhanced the fiction. Here, the people who had left their gas masks at home were afflicted with coughs and streaming eyes, as the gas took effect. At Plummer Roddis, every Monday, 9.15am to 9.45am, customers could expect to be served by staff wearing gas masks, as the store's 150 workers, from the managing director downwards, did their drill.

In early May 1941, Hastings launched a War Weapons Week and the town organised all kinds of fund raising schemes. Prime among these were the sale of National Savings stamps and certificates and Defence, Savings and War Bonds. A student at Hastings Art College designed a War Weapons Week savings gauge, which ran the height of the Albert Memorial. There was a fund-raising exhibition of weapons in Robertson Street, including a Messerschmitt cannon shell, which was live and known to be dangerous. During the course of the exhibition, this shell was stolen; the miscreant was requested to return it to the Central Police Station. A local, 'Patriotic Batchelor' offered the gift of a savings certificate to every baby born in the borough during War Weapons Week and one lucky winner was the newly arrived son of Mr and Mrs White. They named him William Winston, in honour of the occasion. The target for the week's savings in Hastings had been set at £200,000 but by Thursday it was exceeded by £64,000. The Home Guard was gaining in stature and, in honour of their first birthday, 14th May, they mounted guard at Buckingham Palace. The HG strength had reached 1,200 battalions and numbered 1,500,000; regulation rifles and American Tommy guns had replaced their makeshift weapons.

On May 24th 1941 the world's biggest battle cruiser, HMS Hood, was hit in the magazine by a single shell from the German battle ship Bismarck. The Hood exploded and sank in four minutes. Only three of the crew of 1,416 survived. Several Hastings men were declared lost or missing on the Hood, one of whom, Marine R. S. Miles, had survived the sinking of the Royal Oak in 1939. The Royal Navy took its revenge, when it sank the Bismarck three days later. In July, one of the Hood's three survivors, Ronald Davis, made an official visit to Hastings.

The misery of the raids on Hastings continued. Joyce Brewer said, "We had one raid in 1941 that I will never forget. It was a June night when noise and bright lights wakened the whole family. A German plane had dropped about 200 incendiary bombs all around us. Our house escaped but Dad extinguished a fire in next-door's roof, another neighbour, poor Mr Brown was terrified, when a bomb bounced down his stairs. The garages along the road were set on fire, destroying all the furniture stored inside and fires were burning all around the vegetable allotments. Luckily, the plane dropped no high explosives. Next morning my brother went out to dig up incendiary bomb fins, which he sold to his mates". A Mr G. C. Taylor, who was taking shelter in a hut during the incendiary raid, was struck on the shoulder, when a bomb pierced the roof of the hut. He was seriously burned but was helped by the courage of Mr F A Easter, who went to his aid, extinguished the fire and suffered badly burned hands as a result. Following this terrifying raid, a huge exercise was mounted in Hastings by the civil defence services, which involved not only local fire fighters but also those from Bexhill, Battle, Eastbourne and Hailsham. It was presumed for the purposes of the exercise that a squadron of enemy aircraft had attacked the town with high explosives and incendiary bombs and damaged the water mains.

Late June brought a hint of normality to Hastings when parts of the beach were opened, between 7.30am to sunset, for sea bathing. No doubt in an attempt to save on heating and water, a man was observed in the sea, lathering his body with a bar of soap. The opening of the beaches resulted in a tragedy at Marina, when a local man and his daughter were drowned, whilst swimming in rough sea conditions, which, in peacetime, would have been signalled by red warning flags. Food regulations continued to dominate the news on the home front; the Ministry of Agriculture exhorted people to follow the food code and to have no waste food in the home and not to try and wangle a little extra meat ration. The Ministry of Food requested that meat should not be displayed in shop windows, to avoid contamination by flying glass in air raids. Rymills the Butchers, of Kings Road, went one better and assured customers that their meat was stored in gas-proof refrigerators. Rymills also had their shop shutters painted with artistic pictures of sides of meat and strings of sausages, to compensate for the empty windows. The enterprising Lifeboat Restaurant in the Old Town advertised, "Save your meat ration-tasty fish dinners from one shilling (5p).

Hastings Corporation relented on the matter of beetroot instead of blossoms in the town's decorative flowerbeds; red and yellow tulips made a cheering sight round the town centre's Albert Memorial clock tower and geraniums were planted in the seafront gardens. The Women's Land Army recruits were pictured in the local paper, happily cultivating the Red Lake Recreation Ground. 'They used to have less interesting jobs as typists, cinema usherettes and domestic servants', ran the propaganda. The Maidstone and District Service employed the first bus conductress in the locality, the attractive Miss Jean Playford, of Northiam. Her newspaper photograph also seemed like part of a recruiting campaign; neatly uniformed, she managed to look both businesslike and alluring, standing on the bus platform, grasping her ticket machine!

On June 1st came the surprise introduction of clothes rationing. Until the proper ration cards could be distributed, people had to use their margarine coupons for clothes. Every person in Great Britain was allocated a maximum of just 66 clothing coupons per annum. This allowed for one complete outfit a year but a clothing ration could be given up to another person. Second hand clothes were not rationed so there was a rush on the shops that sold these. In 1942, a further control was introduced, a utility scheme, to limit the amounts of material used in the making of clothes. Men's suits were permitted no more than three pockets and three buttons, no trouser turn-ups and 18 inch maximum trouser leg width. Women's skirts were not allowed elastic waistbands or fancy belts and shoes were not to be manufactured with heels higher than two inches.

Examples of clothing coupons needed to buy certain garments:
1. Woman's nightdress. 6 coupons.
2. Woman's dress. 16 coupons.
3. Man's overcoat.16 coupons.
4. Man's underpants. 4 coupons.
5. Pyjamas. 8 coupons.
6. One handkerchief. ½ coupon.
7. Two ounces of knitting wool. 2 coupons.

It's not clear if patriotism or a sense of humour came into play, when the ensembles worn at a Hastings, post-clothing ration wedding were described as follows: 'The bride was attired in a dress to the value of a year's margarine coupons and the bridesmaids contributed 44 coupons for their own dresses. The bride's mother gave 25 coupons. The bridegroom, looking smart in his cricket flannels, gave all his clothing coupons to buy a present of lingerie for the bride, whose going away outfit was a blue costume that had been given a visit to the cleaners'. On the home front, people were told

that they could do much to help the war effort with 'Make do and Mend'. The Board of Trade issued leaflets detailing every aspect of prolonging the life of apparel and household textiles. Women were told to join a make do and mend class or start one of their own. The aim was to avoid using new textiles, in order to make more available for needs of national importance.

Importation of cotton and linen put a strain on merchant shipping, which was already occupied with bringing in life's necessities. Cotton was an important textile in war munitions so household cottons and linens became harder to replace. Many women adopted the thrifty housewife's practice of turning bed sheets, worn thin in the centre, 'sides to middle'. Old sheets had special potential for re-cycling. One ingenious lady claimed that from a few worn out bed sheets she made her husband, 'two shirts, six soft collars, six pairs of shorts, and twelve handkerchiefs'. At that time, flour and dog biscuits were still being sold in little cotton sacks and it was suggested that these could be unpicked, washed and used as cloths for boiled puddings or children's handkerchiefs. (Not mutual use, one hopes!)

Hints for laundering techniques abounded; particularly necessary in the care of Rayon; known as artificial silk and the 'luxury' fabric of the poorer classes. It was flexible and hard wearing when dry but during washing it temporarily lost almost half its strength, it could not be wrung in case it fell apart. Rayon stockings were also made but these tended to bag and sag, as did the thicker lisle (polished cotton) stockings; all were on coupons and in time, difficult to come by. Pure silk stockings disappeared almost completely. If a pair of these was in the possession of an unscrupulous man they became a persuasive currency. Nylon stockings arrived later on in the war, brought over by American servicemen. (Read as for silk stockings)!

Wool was required in wartime for uniforms as well as for other purposes so new, pure woollen clothing for civilians became almost unavailable. Wool was regarded at that time as having therapeutic qualities and with the unheated British homes and damp, chilly climate there was much to be said for that view. Every scrap of wool was carefully used and the repair and reuse of old socks became an obsession. Worn out socks could be unravelled, to replace scarce darning wool; the toes of socks were darned with odds and ends of non-matching wool. An ingenious suggestion for the use of old socks was to turn them into small gloves or mittens, creating a pattern by drawing round the hand. Any remaining fragments of the sock were kept for patching yet more socks! Patched clothing was no longer a stigma but an emblem of patriotism. Wasting clothing or textiles was regarded as being as detrimental to the war effort. As the war continued, high prices, shortages or the lack of coupons made it more difficult to buy new shoes and some took to mending their own, a skill

that had been commonplace in working class homes for generations. There were children's shoe exchange schemes, to put out-grown footwear to good use.

Ministry of Information posters told women that keeping smart and attractive was good for the nation's morale during wartime. Fashion starved women turned their hand to what was surely the peak of make do and mend- remaking one garment into another. Women's magazines printed articles and pattern booklets, which gave instructions on how to convert garments; a man's suit

'Convert a man's suit to a woman's costume'.
Source: Unknown

into a woman's costume, a petticoat into a baby gown or a tennis dress into a pair of knickers and a blouse; the alternatives seemed endless.

The increase in home knitting was not just to make clothing but as a hobby to pass the hours spent in air raid shelters. There was a shortage of knitting patterns and many were painstakingly hand copied. The shortage of dress fabrics, coupled with government imposed design regulations created the fashion that we now see as typically forties; shorter skirts, tighter, minimally-trimmed jackets, square, padded shoulders and plain hats; almost like a military uniform and befitting a nation

1940's knitting pattern.

at war. Hairstyles changed to short or upswept, to accommodate a military service cap or the protective headgear of a munitions worker. Shampoo was soon in short supply as were toiletries and cosmetics. The only face powder was in one pale shade, 'natural' and lipstick, when it was available, was bright red, creating the forties 'femme fatale' image.

Also affected by shortages were other goods like furniture and, as people couldn't replace or repair their house contents, homes grew shabbier as the war continued. A limited supply of utility furniture was produced, with designs that used as little wood and other raw materials as possible. This furniture was allocated to newlyweds only, or to people who had lost everything in a bombing raid. Designs and materials for the manufacture of everyday items like crockery, saucepans and umbrellas were also strictly controlled and the quantities of the goods limited. There were even controls on the manufacture of sewing cotton, safety and dressmaking pins and hair dressing accessories, such as combs, hairgrips, metal curlers and hairpins. In July 1941, the rationing of coal and coke began and only one ton of any fuel per month was permitted for domestic use. This restriction also applied to hotels, offices and clubs. Coal production was falling because of the call up of young miners and the 50,000 ex-miners seemed unwilling to answer Ernest Bevin's appeal to come forward.

The Ministry of Food recommendation was that people should eat one pound of potatoes every day. The price of potatoes was pegged at

a penny a pound, year round and 'Doctor Carrot' and 'Potato Pete' put in their first appearance in MOF posters. Much emphasis was placed on the nutritional potential of British grown, root vegetables and 'appetising' recipes, which included these, either as a main ingredient or a substitute, began to appear.

To boost national morale, a campaign was mounted to promote the Victory V sign. The WVS sold labels bearing the V sign, for one penny each, to display in house or shop windows. The proceeds were to buy munitions. People vied with each other to find different ways of interpreting the defiant sign; errand boys painted it on their bikes, girls drew it on their faces with an eyebrow pencil and gardeners planted out beds in a V. Mr J Beeching of 59 Clifton Road, proudly displayed a V-shaped potato that had grown on his allotment. This may all seem very fatuous now but it was an effective psychological weapon, an emblem of faith and hope that spread widely, linking the free peoples of the world. The Hastings WVS announced that the initial sales of their V for Victory labels had raised twelve pounds ten shillings. In August 1941, the propaganda film, Target for Tonight, was shown in Hastings over a period of three days, to full houses. This fifty-minute film, made by the Crown Film Unit, with the co-operation of the Royal Air Force, was the authentic story of a bombing raid on Germany, showing how it was planned and carried out. The film was about bomber "F for Freddie" on a typical raid mission to a German oil store depot; it also showed how the RAF was organized. Everyone seen in the picture was a member of the RAF, re-enacting their real life roles for the film, from the Commander-in-Chief to the aircraft crew. Its style was one of typical British understatement, which emphasised the dramatic climax. It won an Academy Award for Best Documentary Feature in 1941. A local film making club had recently been established by a budding Hastings photographer, George Ivan Barnett, aged 16. He had started to make a patriotic film called 'There'll Always be an England', in which he used shots of Hastings civil defence and fire fighters. He intended to make a thirty-minute film, which would cost £20 to complete. It had to be checked by censorship authorities throughout its progress

At the height of summer 1941, Hastings seemed to slip into a pseudo-peacetime mode; the local newspaper found space for such homely items as that of a cucumber that was two feet long and weighed two pounds four ounces, a fine crop of onions was shown in the flower beds at Alexandra Park and the Women's Institute held an immensely popular sale of home produce, including a few, quickly sold chickens. Hastings Magistrate Court saw the usual parade of offenders; curfew breakers, those caught without identity cards and retailers and customers who had flouted rationing regulations. More seriously, there were court appearances by looters of bombed buildings. The most frequent cases in court were blackout offenders, who often came up with imaginative excuses. One accused said that her kitten must have turned on a table lamp. The clerk, Colonel F G Langham replied, 'What you think it will do when it is a full grown cat, turn on the seafront lights, I suppose?' (Laughter in court) The accused was fined ten shillings (50p).

Throughout the war, home front life was punctuated by campaign weeks and September brought War Work Week, to persuade Hastings women to become one of the 100,000 women needed by the ATS or to take up munitions work. There were hundreds of enquiries at the ATS exhibition, mounted at the White Rock Pavilion. November 1941 saw the temporary suspension of the ban on coastal visits, a concession that could be cancelled at any time. There were to be no additional transport facilities provided for visitors but the suspension was  welcomed as a tonic for the townspeople, making them feel less isolated. The demands on the time and money of the people of Hastings were unceasing. More Home Guards were needed, another Dig for Victory week was heralded, and a week in March 1942 was declared Warship Week, when, the town was informed, it would be expected to raise money to buy a destroyer! To go along with this, a points system for non-rationed foods was introduced, in effect, an additional form of rationing.

Dear Hannah,

In October 1941 we left Somerset and returned to Chislehurst. My parents quickly found a job, living in and looking after a large house that was owned by a man who was absent. He had spent quite a lot of time abroad, as a hunter and trophy collector. My chief memory of this gloomy, forbidding house is that it had a long, dark staircase and fixed to its wall was a tiger skin, with glaring eyes and open mouth, full of sharp teeth. To add to the terror, there was a huge, stuffed bear waiting at the head of the stairs, with its paws extended. It's no wonder I have no recollection of air raids during this period, when my overriding fear was of nightly creeping past these ferocious animals on my way to bed. My favourite place on this property was the orchard. Sitting there, reading a book and eating the windfall apples kept me happy for hours. My two brothers had found work, Derrick at Kolster Brandes and Ron in the bake house at the Marlborough Bakeries in Sidcup. My parent's job as live-in caretakers provided us with a home but we knew it was just a temporary situation; the house owner returned and we had to go. We went to live with my father's sister Aunt Kit, a short, plump, full-bosomed woman, with a bossy strut, which I used to imitate. Divine Justice has been at work and I believe that in my old age I look just like her! She was rather sharp-tongued but her husband was a big, kindly, slow-speaking country-man. I adored him. Their home was a flat, above a shop, just opposite Chislehurst Library. What luck for this greedy reader! We finally found a home of our own, on a housing estate that had been under construction when war was declared. The building contract was abandoned, leaving unmade roads and some partially completed houses. We moved into 27, Walden Avenue, some time before Christmas, expecting very little joy from the festive season. Wartime conditions ensured that Christmas food treats were out of the question. Sweets were rationed and British grown apples and pears were the only fruits available. There would probably have been beer, my father's family were keen beer drinkers, but if wines or spirits were available, their price put them beyond the reach of my family. My mother hoarded what little she could from our rations, to make some semblance of a Christmas pudding. What would she have done without grated carrots, the un-rationed dates or some gravy browning, for the bulk and colour in the 'plum duff'? I cannot remember what meat we had, but I expect that the gravy, my mother's forte, was excellent.

There were no Christmas trees available; land was needed to grow food. At school, to serve as a tree, we painted bare twigs with white distemper, decorated them with twists of coloured paper and stuck them in a bucket of sand. It was probably one of the many emergency *fire buckets, kept all over the school, ready to smother burning incendiary bombs. Last Christmas, in a florist's shop, I saw bunches of white painted twigs, fixed in an aluminium bucket, selling at £18. Can you wonder that I laughed out loud?*

Providing Christmas presents was a real challenge and as the effects of the war grew, even the most ordinary items became acceptable gifts. Today you would look askance at a packet of razor blades, one tablet of scented soap, a comb, a packet of hairgrips or a torch battery as a Christmas present, but in 1941 these often represented a sacrifice on the part of the giver. It was almost an advantage to be a poor family in wartime. We were already used to doing without and making the best of what we had. The creating of homely Christmas presents flourished, in spite of the increasing shortage of raw materials. Make-do-and-mend was my mother's speciality. After dress fabric became rationed, two of the few materials off coupons were surgical lint and cotton wool. She made these into welcomed gifts; wash cloths, powder puffs, stuffed toys and even baby garments. These were all attractively soft, until laundering rendered them thin and scratchy.

My brother Ron was good at watercolour painting and he turned out calendars, made of a sheet of card, on which he drew and painted a Disney cartoon character. The card was liberally sprinkled with glued-on glitter and a penny calendar was attached. He was even taking orders for these, (sixpence a time), as was my mother, for her inventive needlework. It was a happy interlude, sitting at the table with my brother, giving him a hand with cutting and gluing and listening to the radio, my favourite entertainment after books. After I had gone to bed, my mother secretly set about creating a wonderful Christmas present for me, out of cast offs. She had managed to get hold of a discarded dolls pram and had given it a good clean. She unpicked two old jumpers, one red, one pink, and various other discarded garments. She used the materials to make complete outfits for my two shabby dolls and two sets of pillows, blankets and covers for the pram. It was overwhelming to wake on that Christmas morning and discover this unexpected present, all the more precious because it was my familiar and dearly loved dolls that were arrayed in such finery.

Love From Gran'ma

In Hastings, two hundred local families received goods from a real life Father Christmas, who for the past few years, had been giving deserving cases seasonal gifts of coal and food. This anonymous benefaction continued, until an obituary notice in January 1949 revealed his name as Mr W H Langdon. For most people Christmas 1941 promised to be a bleak affair, as the effects of war kept families apart and food rationing and other shortages dampened the festive spirit.

1942

Scrap metal was becoming vital to the war effort and in the New Year, the obsolete tramlines along the Ridge were excavated; they provided 240 tons of salvage. A relic of a former war was also called into service. A trophy, Russian cannon, along with its carriage and ammunition, yielded four tons of scrap. The cannon, which had been captured at the siege of Sebastopol in the Crimean War, had stood opposite to the seafront Pelham Crescent for 70 years; it was eventually moved to the grounds of Hastings Museum. A Mr Gabb wrote to the local paper saying that he was born in Wellington Square, Hastings, during the siege of Sebastopol and remembered, during his childhood, seeing the trophy cannon occasionally fired out to sea. Also dismantled and scrapped in 1942, were the gates and front railings of Alexandra Park. Householders were told that the railings from one domestic frontage could make 100 rifle barrels and those from 160 houses, a tank.

Removing Alexandra Park gates for salvage. Source: HSLO

Today's recycling schemes seem feeble compared with those organised in WWII. Hastings' Mayor launched a waste paper drive and the town entered a national competition for collecting the greatest quantity in a month. Clean waste paper had many wartime uses, including the manufacture of cardboard for cartridges, shell linings, rings, wads and washers for shells and boxes for detonators. Between 1st and 31st January, Hastings collected 240 tons of waste paper and won a prize of £50, coming joint third in a contest with 1, 234 British towns and cities. The country amassed a total of 100, 000 tons of waste paper.

Because of the secrecy that necessarily surrounded the official visits of important personages during the war, it is sometimes difficult to verify facts. Noel Care told of a visit to Hastings by His Majesty King George

VI. The only mention of a royal visit was in the Hastings and St Leonards Observer dated 6th July 1940: 'King George VI passed through a SE coast town (the censorship-imposed description of Hastings) on Monday afternoon...drove the length of the seafront, during a tour of inspection of a large section of the south-east coast'. However, Noel's account mentions weather conditions that indicate that this report was not the visit he witnessed. "It was a cold winter morning, at a time when the threat of invasion was foremost in our minds. I was delivering a grocery order to a flat in Verulam place, above the Information Centre. While going down White Rock Road, I was stopped by a police inspector, who was accompanied by three soldiers with fixed bayonets. He told me if I delivered the groceries I would have to stay at the flat until mid-day, as the King was coming to inspect the troops. I was only allowed to pass through because the police inspector knew me and the customer was an important Hastings lady. Flanked by two Guardsmen I was allowed to watch from a window. The wait was fairly lengthy and the troops kept marking time and doing rifle drill, to keep warm. It was interesting to see the King and the several generals, even though I did not know who they were".

Dear Hannah,

We settled down in our new home in Walden Avenue. The street had an unfinished feel about it; the roads and pavements had been abandoned unmade and these became a muddy stream in wet weather, very unkind to ill-shod feet as mine were by then. My mother and I began a friendship with a neighbouring mother and her little girl, who was the same age as me. The mother did all the things mine didn't, she smoked, wore make up, and tight-fitting clothes and, most glamorous of all, she cleaned the house of Mantovani, the famous bandleader. My mother had two cleaning jobs in Holbrook Lane, for a doctor and a stockbroker, not professions that carried much weight in the schoolyard boasting stakes! My father had several gardening jobs and Double British Summer time enabled him to work late into the evenings. He too had a famous customer, Stuart Hibbard, the BBC Home Service radio announcer. Another gardening job he had was for a man whose wife perpetually wore bedroom attire. She would walk about the garden in her negligee, instructing my father on her horticultural requirements. He found this immodesty insulting, being, as I have said, always concerned with 'what's right!' Derrick joined the navy and suddenly, without his exuberant outbursts, the house was quieter. I had such a contrasting pair of brothers, Derrick provided wild excitement at times but Ron was the steady and kindly influence. He was the one certainty in a period of family upheaval. Derrick's departure seemed to trigger worsened relations between my parents. My father took refuge in the pub, to return home at closing time to find my mother ready for yet another argument. These raged in my hearing, as I was still awake, full of apprehension for the violent row that was sure to come. The stress, added to the fears and deprivations of war, caused my always-clear skin to break out into scabby sores on my face and body and set me on a distressing round of medical consultations, including one at Guy's Hospital in London. My worst fear was that my face would be painted with the highly coloured, gentian violet, a remedy for dermatitis, thus marking me as 'unclean' at school.

For health and war emergency reasons, my schooling continued to be a spasmodic affair, so I resorted to the comforting routine of self-education at the kitchen table. My mother had to work and I would either take my books to the house where she was cleaning or stay at home alone, listening to the BBC Home Service or reading our family 'library', This consisted of the few books my father had bought on instalments; Arthur Mee's Children's Encyclopaedia, a set of Daily Express dictionaries and a collection of domestic, 'How To' volumes, published by Odhams Press in 1934. From these I learned about gardening, first aid, common ailments and anatomy, running a home, how to deal with family problems (!) and how to entertain at home. The book entitled 'How to Write, Think and Speak Correctly' set my style for life! There was nothing on arithmetic and my understanding of numbers remained undeveloped. My father tried to teach me to tell the time, a process that was as frustrating to me as it was to him and his short-tempered impatience was a considerable disadvantage in the process. No one then had heard of dyscalculia, a condition that has dogged me all my life.

With Very much Love, Gran'ma.

1942

Ivor White joined the Home Guard in January 1942 He said, "I don't know why I waited until just after my 15th birthday to apply, because I was going to lie about my age anyway. Ironically, the day I decided to go to their HQ to enlist, there was my Headmaster, Mr Clarke, sitting in reception, waiting to do the same thing". In common with thousands of boys all over the country, Ivor was a keen war souvenir collector and, being very enterprising, he used to chase enemy aircraft that were obviously in trouble and about to crash. He said, "Many came down near my home but I remember one that came down a bit further off. Word travelled quickly in those days, even though we never owned a telephone, and I was told that a Heinkel 111 had crashed at Cripp's Corner. I got on my bike and pedalled like mad to reach the scene, before the authorities began to clear up. The field where the twin-engine bomber had crashed was littered with debris and I soon found some aluminium tubing, which I later made into decorative finger-rings and cigarette lighters.

The White Family. Boy Home Guard, Ivor extreme right.

It was at this crash that I made my first gruesome discovery of the war. I found an airman's boot, with a section of lower-leg still inside. It was a great shock to a youngster but there were far worse incidents to follow in my service life with the Irish Guards and I became almost immune to such horrors. As a boy Home Guard, I was being trained to kill; we were brain washed into thinking that sticking a bayonet into a straw-stuffed sack was going to win the war so, my reasoning was that for every enemy plane that crashed, there would be less of the enemy that I would have to kill with my bayonet.

My salvage collection included many panel instruments from aircraft, ammunition, and two complete 20mm cannons. All of the ammunition was rendered harmless by extracting the bullet and emptying the cordite from the cartridges. The detonator caps were then exploded, while held in a vice, using a hammer and a nail, before re-assembling

71

1942

and polishing the complete items for display. I had no fear of guns and explosives in those days as I had been using a 12-bore shotgun since I was big enough to hold one to my shoulder. Grandfather always kept a gun, already loaded, in the scullery. Safety-catch on, of course!

Crashed German aircraft. Source: Ivor White.

When my brother and I first 'acquired' those 20mm cannons we decided to hide them in the attic of our Senlac Gardens home, until the debris of the crashed aircraft had been cleared. They might have still been in the attic until this day, had it not been for the local policeman, who lived next door but one, telling my Mum that the authorities were looking for people who had visited the crash scene. This was probably a friendly warning, to the effect that if her boys had removed anything they should get rid of it. It was well known that 'our gang' were avid souvenir collectors. Needless to say, Mum put her foot down and the guns had to go. We greased them up and wrapped them in a sack and my brother went out that night, with another member of the gang and dumped them in a small, deep murky pond, to join the frilly-backed, black and orange newts that we loved to catch with a worm, tied to a piece of string".

Warship Week was the next challenge to the Hastings fundraisers. The local paper organised a town-wide darts match, the Irish Guard's boxing champion, Arthur Danahur, came to town to give an exhibition of the Noble Art at the White Rock Pavilion. There was 'Unique Variety Entertainment' bill, which boasted 'Talent from London's Air Raid Shelters', including 'Jimmy Nix, with a thrill from the Home Guard!' All this, combined with a tremendous efforts from groups and individuals, raised £352,000.

Soap rationing came into force on 9th February, with the cutting of supplies by 20%, to save imported oils for food rations. This new form of rationing was supposed be remain a secret until it was officially announced but somehow people got wind of it and there was a run on stocks. The ration was four ounces of household soap and two ounces of toilet soap, soap flakes or chips per person per month.

A Hastings Magistrate publicly despaired of the state of affairs in local schooling, commenting on the amount of children roaming the streets and getting into mischief and petty crime. A survey revealed that apart from those attending private schools, there were only 2,700 local children in education, for just three hours a day. Throughout the war, the Hastings Courts saw the usual procession of petty criminals, but with a reduction of cases of drunkenness. There were only 23 in the previous year and '18 of these were non-residents', as the Observer's 'Vigilant' primly commented.

Many offences that came to court were war-related. Reading these, one can only conclude that during the war, Great Britain must have been the most regulated free country. Infringement of emergency rulings such as blackout failure, curfew breaking and not carrying an identity card continued and almost always incurred a fine. Looting bombed buildings was regarded as a very serious crime and it carried a sentence of 14 years penal servitude, as did black marketeering. Theft of hard to come by goods and the waste of food and other materials that affected the war effort were also taken very seriously, as may be gathered from the following examples: 'Pub licensees throughout the country were complaining that drinking glasses were disappearing in their thousands and they felt offenders should be fined or sent to prison', said Mr Harold Glenister, the prosecuting solicitor at Hasting Police Court, acting on behalf of the Licensed Victualler's Association. Before the court was a local woman, who had walked out of the King's Head Pub at Ore, taking with her a glass, half-filled with beer, when 'time' was called. The licensee gave chase and apprehended the woman. The said glass, produced in court, was valued at one shilling (5p). The magistrate decided to make an example of her and she was fined two pounds or 14 days in prison. Hastings saw its first prosecution for wasting food in March 1942, when a couple were accused of committing the offence, during a period of 60 days. The waste, produced in court as evidence, consisted of bread, galantine, (meat loaf) fruit cake, scones, muffins and tins of milk, all discovered in the dustbin of the offenders. In their defence, the couple said they were frequently away from home and also ate out a lot. As there was not an efficient system for the collection of waste for pigs, they had put the stale food in the dustbin. The husband was fined two pounds and the wife three.

This next example of wartime regulations beggars belief but it could have been the starting point of the British obsession with queuing. In April 1942, the government issued an order that when more than six people were waiting for a bus, a queue must be formed. The Hastings and St Leonards Observer published a pair of helpful photographs, illustrating the right and wrong ways to wait for a bus. In May, Hastings had its first prosecution under these new regulations. It was stated that a woman, 'took up her position in a queue otherwise than behind the last person forming that queue'. After the magistrate pointed out that the maximum sentence for this crime was a fine of £100 or three months in prison, the case was dismissed, with the warning that future offenders would not be treated so lightly. Hastings residents protested. With several trolleybuses buses drawing up at one pickup point simultaneously and the mechanical impossibility of these vehicles to negotiate parking spots, confusion often arose about who was waiting for which bus. The Hastings Police said the regulation with reference to queuing would have to be reconsidered.

The role of women in the war effort was tremendous and to recognise this and encourage more women to follow suit, the Hastings and St Leonards Observer ran a series of articles called Women and the War, with photographs depicting women doing what had traditionally been a man's job. One woman, whose husband had gone into making munitions, took over his window-cleaning round and ran it with another woman, providing a service to shops, houses and the Royal East Sussex Hospital. The two women were nicknamed the Two Georges, a reference to the popular and slightly risqué George Formby song, 'When I'm Cleaning Windows'. The Post Office took on and trained female engineers; one, who was formerly employed in a clothing outfitter's showrooms, was working in maintenance control, testing lines, while others learned fitting. A woman who had been a milk round worker in WWI became a goods porter at the railway station; she said that she enjoyed the job. Three women working in a Queen's Road butcher's shop earned themselves the title, 'The Sausage Queens' They said, "We do more than make sausages, we serve customers and chop up carcasses and we each still have ten fingers left!" These 'butcheresses' were very popular with the housewives.

The government offered a six-week training course, as factory canteen staff, to the female cooks in the Hastings now almost redundant hotels and guesthouses. In March, conscription was extended to men up to 45 and women aged between 20 and 30. There was also a war registration scheme for girls of 16 and 200,000 girls signed up for this, including Princess Elizabeth. By the November of 1942 bus conductresses on Hastings trolley buses were an every day sight. Young George Ivan Barnett was still busy with the making of his film, 'There'll Always be an England'. This created some extraordinary scenes on The Ridge, as locals saw a swastika-marked German motor cycle and enemy shock troops, armed with hand grenades, Tommy guns and rifles, going into action against 'Polish' peasants.

The Hastings Women Voluntary Service continued its wide-ranging work. They trained women for a Housewives' Service, under which women offered their own homes as emergency accommodation and as feeding and first aid centres. Probably due to censorship, the only public recognition of the arrival of hundreds of Canadian troops in Hastings was the newspaper announcement, in April, that the WVS was setting up a new social club for Canadian forces. Canadian troops had begun to arrive in Great Britain towards the end of 1939 and records show that 500,000 Canadian armed services personnel spent some of their service in Britain. There were 40,000 British/Canadian marriages and 7,000 to 8,000 of these Canadians settled in Sussex after the war. Noel Care recalled that the first large contingent of Canadians were stationed in empty hotels and other abandoned properties. "These friendly young men were very popular with locals", he said. Many of the Canadian servicemen left Hastings in early August, prior to the Dieppe commando raids.

Joyce Brewer said: "A Canadian crew arrived and mounted their gun just a few yards from our house, overlooking the valley, where the power and railway station were sited. The first time the gun was fired it broke one of our windows. They were a lovely bunch of lads and although they never hit any planes, it was great to have them there, it gave us a feeling of security". Joyce remembers a

Broomgrove Valley Power Station
Source: Richard H Maynard

particularly terrible raid on May 3rd. "It was 9.00pm, a beautiful evening and still light because of British Double Summertime. I was just going up to bed, with a bundle of comics and a glass of milk. Suddenly, there was the sound of planes and looking out of the front door I saw these four single-engine fighters heading towards us very fast. Thinking they were ours, I stayed to give them a wave. They were not ours. One dropped a bomb on Emmanuel Church, killing the vicar's baby and the other three machine-gunned and dropped their bombs up near Ore Village. One came in so low I could actually see the pilot and every mark and rivet on the plane. If he had fired his cannon I wouldn't be here now".

Noel Care was on duty that night, attending the scene of the bombing at The Broadway in Ore Village. He carried out first aid on the seriously and slightly injured and waited for the Rescue Services to dig out two elderly women, who were buried in the ruins of their shop. As he waited, a very anxious man from a nearby house approached; his daughter had been locked in the bathroom when the bomb fell and she did not respond when he called her. Noel said, "Three of us went with him

Canadian serviceman, Doug Powell.

immediately and kicked the bathroom door in and found the unconscious girl in the bath, her face just above the icy water. The ceiling had collapsed and pieces of it had struck her head. Finding no obvious injuries, we then had to lift her out of the bath, a difficult job, even though we had a mechanical lifting device. She obviously recovered from her ordeal, as I saw her walking in the town several weeks later. I returned to the ruined shop, to find the only duty we could carry out was to remove the two women, both were dead".

Joyce's family soon made friends with the Canadians, but most particularly with Doug Powell, aged 18, from Nova Scotia. Her Mum made all the soldiers welcome; she used to sew on their battledress stripes and flashes, darn their socks and give them meals from the family's meagre rations. Joyce's Dad used to let the soldiers come into the house for a game of billiards, on a quarter-sized billiard table, which also served as an indoor refuge during air raids, until their Morrison Shelter was delivered. The Canadians eventually left and British gun crews took over and stayed until the latter end of 1944. Both of Joyce's sisters married soldiers, Jack and Jim, who were billeted in their road.

Of food rationing Joyce Brewer said, "My mother never professed to be a marvellous cook but during the war we never went hungry, despite the severe rationing we always had good, substantial meals. Dad kept a dozen chickens and some rabbits, as many as 50 at times. He also worked hard on five allotments, so we always had a wide variety of fresh vegetables. It still took ingenuity to make the best of things and Mum worked wonders with what she had. I particularly remember her sausage meat pie, delicious, served cold with tomatoes and salad. My Dad would put large potatoes in the ashes under our coal fire and many a night we had them for supper, with a small pat of butter and pepper and salt. Dried egg was an ingredient that produced many good meals; cooked as an omelette and served with tomato sauce, it made a satisfying dish. So were Mum's bacon fritters, made of just one rasher of bacon, cut into tiny pieces, mixed with potatoes and a beaten egg and cooked in a frying pan. When apples were scarce, Mum added marrow and a clove, we had many an apple pudding made like this. When she could get some dried fruit, Mum made 'Spotted Dog', boiled in a cloth or she produced jam or treacle pudding, steamed in a basin. The fact that we were a family of six helped, because Mum had more portions of rationed food to work with but she still had to be careful. She scraped every trace of margarine and lard from their greaseproof wrappings and then used the paper to line cake tins. Because my Dad worked on the railways he got a ration of pies but these were not very good. The pastry was rock hard and the meat scant and gristly. We had these with mashed potatoes and red cabbage, which we used to eat with closed eyes, because we could not stand the colour. When the meat ran out, we would have cauliflower or macaroni cheese, in which my mother would put layers of sliced tomato. I disliked saccharine tablets, which we used to supplement the sugar ration. If they did not dissolve properly you would find a fragment in your mouth; it had a horrible metallic taste".

Joyce's mention of sausage meat pie is supported by two of the never-ending announcements from the Ministry of Food. Firstly, that sausages would no longer be made with skins, "Humans are not the only ones to have their overcoats rationed", went the government quip. Secondly, the arrival of tinned pork sausage meat from America, promoted in the MOF advertisements by a 'Mrs Merry', a big, homely woman, whose hefty forearms were folded over the usual floral pinafore. Mrs Merry said she had been eating well on the tinned sausage meat: 'One and a half pounds of pure pork in its own gravy, with a generous layer of fat, which can be used for frying or baking'. This tinned meat was 12 food points.

There was no white bread on sale after April 6th; the National Wheatmeal Loaf, which was not brown but off-white in colour, was imposed on the public, in order to save shipping. In spite of promotion by the Ministry of Food, only 7% had taken it up voluntarily. Cuts in clothing ration were also announced, to release 50,000 textile workers for war service. Further restrictions came into force for the manufacture and design of clothing, including a ban on lace and embroidery on underwear. Women were asked to go without stockings in the summer, so that there would be a supply for winter. Some women resorted to staining their legs with gravy browning and then drawing in a seam line up the back of the legs with an eyebrow pencil. Gravy browning is made from caramelised sugar so these 'stockings' could come to a sticky end in a shower of rain.

Ore Children's Great Scrap Metal Effort

The Ore "victory pile" and the boys and girls who made it. Note the Union Jack on top.

The Church Street Kids scrap pile. Source: HSLO

The drive for salvage continued and in June, Hastings Corporation erected a notice, asking people to place scrap metal at certain points, including on the green at the junction of Greville Road and Church Street, Ore Village. Local children seemed to think, 'This means us', and set about gathering every bit of scrap metal in the area. The pile included bedsteads, tins, bicycle frames, bedsprings, buckets, fenders, sheets of metal, cisterns and even a car chassis. They had collected these items from the valley behind the streets, from neighbouring houses and gardens. In four days they had gathered enough scrap to fill three Corporation lorries. On one of the sheets of metal the kids had painted, 'To Adolf Hitler, from Ore' and it was set on top of the pile, along with the Union Jack. The local authority employed female scrap metal locators, who worked under a supervisor, who the newspaper skittishly dubbed, 'Miss Locator'. The women went to garages, work's yards, forges and farms. Among their finds were a disused steam roller, a huge cast iron cauldron used for dipping hop poles and a cattle trough that formed part of an old marine mine. Even the bones from the scant meat rations were valuable. There was a twice- monthly collection of bones, as they had many uses; as glue, soap, crop fertilizers and for grinding into a flour, to bulk-out the cattle food. The cartridge of each shell had a firing charge made from the glycerine in bones.

Dear Hannah,

After having been employed as a jobbing gardener, Ron began work in gentleman's outfitters on Royal Parade in Chislehurst. Businesses were obliged to provide their own fire watchers, so the shopkeepers of the parade organised a group from among their workers. Ron was enlisted to do a duty, for which he was paid the generous sum of 3/6 per night. His evening duty sometimes began with a pint or two and a few games of snooker with his fire watching mate at the Bull Inn. Afterwards, they went back to a room above a shop, enjoyed a can of soup they had brought along and then set up camp beds, hoping for a peaceful night.

Ron returned home one morning, to our anxious mother, who asked him if he had heard the heavy air raid and the tremendous explosion but they had not. In fact, they had both slept soundly the entire night. They learned later that day that an anti-aircraft gun had hit the bomb bay of a German plane as it flew over Chislehurst. The force of the explosion had thrown shrapnel, bits of aeroplane and body parts over a huge area. They did not mention having slept through all of this while on fire watching duty but it was no more pre-duty pints from then on.

My brother Derrick came home on leave from the Royal Navy and how the uniform suited him; the blue was the perfect foil for his dark-blond, wavy hair and fresh complexion. His nickname aboard ship was Rosie. He burst in the back door, sweeping my mother off her feet; only he could

Able Seaman, Derrick Burkin,

make her laugh and cry in equal measure. His various girlfriends began to appear and I viewed them with a mixture of little sister jealousy and curiosity, they seemed so grown up and sophisticated, they must have been all of 16 or 17 years. At the time, I understood very little about Derrick's experiences in the navy. He gusted in and out of my life like a visiting celebrity and my strongest memories are of being hugged to his scratchy naval uniform and the things I learned from him about the traditions associated with its style and wearing, as he got himself ready to go out on the town.

One time, when he was going off leave, we went with him to the railway station. As a child I was always singing, and as we waited on the platform, I ran through my repertoire of sentimental, WWII songs, till Derrick asked my mother to tell me to shut up. I was too young to understand the connection between departure to war and the popular songs of the day. Now I can see that, 'We'll Meet Again', was probably a bit too much for him to bear.

With Very Much Love, from Gran'ma.

In June 1942, Monica reached her 14th birthday: "It was a Thursday and I left school next day and started work on the Saturday, in the village shop, where my older sister also worked; I was utterly thrilled to be taken on. My working day began at 8.00am and ended at 7.00pm, with an hour off at lunchtime; my wage was ten shillings per week. There was a lot to learn, as food rationing was quite fully established. Butter supplies arrived at the shops in huge blocks that had to be cut and weighed up into rations. Lard also came in large blocks; margarine was the only pre-packed item. The cheese, mostly New Zealand Cheddar, came in 80-pound rounds in wooden crates, too heavy for me to handle. I learned how to cut up a side of bacon and bone it out and it wasn't long before I cut myself; I still bear the scar, over sixty years on. I was perfectly happy working in the village shop except for one thing, the Post Office part. During the other girl's lunch break I had to take her place. I did not mind dealing with stamps, postal orders or parcels, but I dreaded the incoming telephone calls. Usually an efficient voice would say, 'We have a telegram', and I would be terrified. Surrounding our village were several encampments of Canadian soldiers; many of these had complicated French names and it was difficult for me to write these down. After I had been working in the shop for six months, my uncle/guardian, a kindly and well-meaning bachelor, thought that my brother and I, whose education and social lives were neglected due to the onset of war, would benefit from some time spent on the Buckinghamshire farm of a gentleman friend of his. My brother preceded me to the farm by two months, then a ticket was sent to me and I was told to catch the 9.00am train from Hastings on 1st January 1943".

During June 1942, the town underwent a sobering experience. A full-scale, military, mock invasion exercise was mounted and The Ridge was used as a stronghold and manned with armed troops. Residents had already been issued with government leaflets in June 1940 that gave advice on what to do in the event of an invasion. More than 60 years on, the brave and patriotic words still strike a chill: "Do not run away, you may be exposed to German machine gunning, as the Dutch and Belgians were... report suspicious strangers...do not tell or give the Germans anything... be ready to help our military... think always of your country before you think of yourself ...the best defence of Great Britain is the courage of her men and women". It was reported that Hastings' mock invasion exercise resulted in many lessons learned and a better understanding between the emergency services.

By 1942 Noel Care, then 19, had moved on from his job as a grocer's assistant and was working, by government order, for Strickland's, an agricultural supplies merchant, but he also continued his Civil Defence first aid duties. He spoke of going to a house in Hastings, when he was on duty, to find a terrible scene. Out of respect for surviving family, the location and identifying details have been excluded. "One incident to which we were sent showed the hazards of enemy machine-gunning. During one of our CD practice mornings a German plane flew over, a common occurrence at the time and we paid little attention to it. Then we got a call out. When we arrived at the scene there was a very pale looking ARP Warden looking out for us, he pointed to a house and said, 'Upstairs, it's pretty bad'. We went up to a room where the floor was covered in blood and we found a woman, lying on her back, with her baby daughter beside her. We discovered a small bullet hole in the woman's chest and a very large exit wound in her back, from where all the blood had issued; she was clearly dead. Her child had been lacerated across the stomach and chest and was unconscious but still alive. It was the first time I had seen the injuries a machine gun could inflict. When I got home it took a long time to remove the blood from my clothing- much longer to remove the horror of the occasion from my mind".

At the age of 16, Clifford Highman was working for the railway. He recalls a house on the beach at Cooden, which was the last building as the train left Hastings. This house had a Tudor chimney and a pretty garden and seemed to be a normal dwelling, but it was used to house a six-inch naval gun, concealed behind a camouflage tarpaulin; the house still exists. Clifford had a chance to meet the enemy face to face before he joined the services. Crossing the Pevensey marshes one day, the train, on which he was the fireman, was halted. Clifford said: "A German ME 109 had crashed in a field nearby. The pilot was unharmed and his main reaction was hurt pride. He was six feet tall and blonde, a real Aryan. He had his 'kills' marked on the plane's fuselage and a picture of a naked Winton Churchill, complete with cigar, on the cockpit" Clifford also worked on the ambulance train that went along the coast, picking up Dunkirk casualties and transporting them to a hospital near Southampton. In 1943, at the age of 17, Clifford joined the Royal Navy and saw service in the Far East.

Those who had family or friends overseas were sometimes fortunate enough to receive food parcels and this letter, from the Lavender Cottage collection, draws a picture of food shortages in wartime Hastings.

Lavender Cottage. June 9th 1942.

My Dear Marion

Emilie Crane on Lavender Cottage doorstep.

I can't tell you how delighted I was to receive your lovely parcel this morning; it was a welcome surprise and more than kind of you to send it. I think the things we have most missed here are butter and fruit; all the fats are so scarce and the rations do not allow us much, so we shall now revel in nice bread and butter. As for oranges, the small consignment sent over is reserved for children under six, which is as it should be, therefore, we shall rejoice in the fruit juice.

The tea will be a treat and I am very intrigued with the egg powder and shall try it at the first opportunity. I have scoured Hastings for a saucepan cleaner, how did you think of that? Soap and sugar are of course rationed strictly. I can get saccharine but I do not care much for it-such sickly stuff. The serviettes will be very useful as the paper shortage is acute. Hence the old notepaper I am using.

I do hope the above remarks do not sound as if we are in a bad way; it is only that things are in short supply. Lord Woolton has done very well; we all think that food distribution is better than in the Great War. We do miss some things, naturally, but we expect that in a terrible war. All day the fighters and bombers go over us on their way to France and Germany. They are Canadians, Americans, British, Polish, etc; we know they do some damage. We have had two raids recently, they were not nice and there were a good many casualties. My other friend's sister is an ambulance driver and she tells us some sad stories but everyone here is wonderfully cheerful and none doubt of ultimate victory. We had an exciting time last week when the wounded from the Commando raid on France were brought to the hospital here; I am sorry to say that one died.

I wish I could do more to help but one's age is against it. (She was 71) I took the first aid course and went to help in a First Aid Post but it was so damp I got pleurisy after three months and the doctor would not let me go there again. So I went for an anti-gas course and received a certificate but fortunately the Germans have not resorted to gas. I offered myself for clerical work but they wanted younger people, so I fell back on door-to-door collecting for the National Savings Campaign and that has been successful. One can do knitting of course, but it isn't exciting to knit all the time; some of my pullovers would fit a large-sized giant! The garden is a great joy and we really have done well with vegetables. Well, my dear, I hope you will forgive this rambling on, there is little news to give you and each day is the repetition of another; planes overhead, air raid alerts and wireless news.

Yours affectionately,

Emilie Crane.

1942

In July 1942, the rationing of sweets and chocolate came into force, with adults and children having the same allocation- half a pound for a four-week period. Chocolate was valued at 16 points per pound, penny chocolate bars were one point and two-penny bars, two points. The previous month, American dried egg made its debut on British menus and was accompanied by the usual MOF cookery tips, including that one level tablespoon of powdered egg and two of water made the equivalent of one fresh egg. To mark the 4th July, Hastings' Mayor asked residents to fly the Stars and Stripes and to offer hospitality to any American soldiers in town.

Dear Hannah,

Emilie Crane mentioned in several of her letters that one of her two house companions, Mrs Edith Lake, was secretary to the committee of Catharine House, a St Leonards residential home for invalid women. Emilie did not add that she too was on that committee, long before and throughout the war. I learned about this a few months after Emilie's letters were published in 2002. Local historian, Ray Gladwish, had got hold of the minute book of the Catharine House committee some twenty years previously, when he bought a job lot from a book dealer. He kindly loaned me the Catherine House committee's meeting records. I had already done some research on the home, which is at 57 Church Road, St Leonards. It was established in Victorian times and I discovered a reference to it in a late 19th century edition of 'News and Reviews', a Hastings and St Leonards trade publication. I love the way it is described: 'A Home for Invalid Gentlewomen, a priceless boon to those of limited means, providing them with a charming home and medical attention, at an almost nominal cost'.

I spent hours going through the committee reports, getting a new glimpse into Emilie's and Edith's voluntary work. By September 1939, the committee of Catherine House was dealing with war regulations. On 12th September, the minutes noted that the blackouts for the building had been completed at a cost of £15. This is the only reference made to the declaration of war and the stoical committee agreed that the home's 1939, Christmas outing and treats should, 'carry on as usual', a phrase frequently used in the coming years by the minute's recorder. This was rather a favourite expression of Emilie's and I am sure she helped Edith with the minutes, in fact, I know she wrote them down at times, as I recognised her hand writing.

By July 1940, the decrease in the number of residents was causing considerable concern and the committee sent a letter to the Chief Constable of Hastings to enquire if, under wartime, 'banned area' regulations, it would be permitted to bring in residents from other areas. (He agreed). The use of the home was also offered as an auxiliary hospital or as a rest centre after air raids. Catherine House itself suffered war damage and the 1940 November minutes record that the cost of waterproofing the bombed roof was £18.19.6d. (£18.95½ p) The home's caretaker, Mr Hale, was called up and it was agreed that his wife should take on his job for £2. 00. 8d (£2. 04p) per week, less the government grant that was routinely paid to a soldier's wife and family. In 1942, Miss Surtees, the home superintendent, said she was having difficulties in obtaining domestic and other staff. This was probably due to the higher wages and better opportunities that the war had created for women. In the same way that the beginning of the war was not mentioned in the Catherine House minutes, neither was its end.

We did learn that Hale was demobilised in November 1945 and would return to work in January 1946, on an increased wage of £2.5.00, (£2.25p), plus the previous free board and lodging for his wife and little son. In spite of the shortage of residents and staff and other setbacks associated with the war and its sequel, Catherine House, unlike many similar establishments, survived and today it is a residence for adults with learning disabilities. I have seen Catherine House from the outside only but I like to think of the two Lavender Cottage ladies and the local worthies, dutifully gathering there for their unfailing, monthly meetings.

Very Much Love from Gran'ma.

In 1993, Ted Dyke, a former WWII Canadian soldier, wrote an autobiography called The Ties That Bind. In the 1920s, when Ted was 12 years old, his family emigrated from Britain to Canada. He earned his living as a farm worker and lumberjack but in September 1939, he enlisted in the Canadian Fifth Field Regiment and arrived in Greenock, Scotland in August 1940. He was eventually deployed to Bexhill-on-

1942

Sea, on Channel Watch. Ted's book included Sussex peoples' memories of the Canadian military presence in their communities. His widow has given permission for some of these extracts to be re-published:

'I knew the Canadian boys well. I met them when I used to play the piano at The Hole in the Wall pub in Hastings. I also remember the Dieppe raid; I lost a lot of friends. A bunch of them came in for a drink before leaving; it was so quiet and sad. They were great boys. I am 79 and never stop thinking of them'.
Mrs W. of Hastings.

'I was a fourteen year-old milk van boy at the time. The Canadians used to help me in their time off, driving the van, while I delivered the milk. They were very friendly, always giving me chewing gum'.
Mr L T. of Bexhill.

'In 1940 I was a very naïve 17 year old. I wanted to join the ATS and to do this I falsified my age. I was posted to Hurst Court, on the Ridge in Hastings. There were 400 of us, all very popular with the 'boys from over there'. There was the 'great romance' we all had one. I met Benny at one of those wonderful, wartime dances. He was from Moose Jaw and his mother had been a War Bride in the First World War. On one occasion he sat with me on the moonlit seafront, sharing an orange that was sealed in candle wax and had been sent to him from home. He went off to war and sadly he did not come back to claim me'.
Mrs M J. of Bexhill.

'I was ten years old and my father was the verger at Fairlight Church, Hastings. The Canadians set up an observation post in the church tower. I will always remember the Canadian voices I heard when I arrived home from school. They used to share with us the sugar they received in parcels from Canada. I was very sad when I heard that only a few of them returned from Dieppe'.
Mr B. B. of Hastings.

'I was engaged to a wonderful Canadian from Vancouver but it was not meant to be; he was killed on the Dieppe raid. We loved them all, such happy go-lucky boys. I remember the heavy transport going to the coast, through the village, just before D-Day; we knew that it was the beginning of the end. I am 73 but still get letters from the few who got home safely'.

1942

Mrs M. B. of Hastings
'I remember Clarence McBride, of the Royal Hamilton Light Infantry. He often came to our house, I was ten years old at the time but he was like a big brother to me. He was killed at Dieppe and a soldier came to tell my sister. Clarence was last seen after he had been machine-gunned in both legs. Many years later I went to Dieppe to find his grave and I was shocked to learn that he was only twenty years old-he had seemed much older'.
Mr B. P. of Hastings

'Mum still recalls being woken up in the middle of the night by a loud noise in the street outside our house, in Battle Road, when she peeped out of the window it was a regiment of Canadian soldiers, who were marching to the railway station, to go to war. The steel studs in their boots on the road were making the noise'.
Mrs M. W. of Hastings

Ivor White recalled the Canadians working in the Maidstone & District Bus garage that used to stand at the bottom of Lower Lake in Battle. Ivor quickly made friends with the team of Canadian Army motor mechanics, known as LAD and he helped them, the 8th Canadian Reconnoitre Battalion, to prepare army vehicles, mainly Jeeps, for a 'secret' raid on the French coast. The Jeep's exhaust pipes had to be lengthened and made vertical, and the distributors sealed, to enable the vehicles to drive into the sea from the landing craft, which often meant submersion to a depth of three or four feet in the sea-water. He said: "I met lots of the Canadians billeted in Battle, those smartly dressed soldiers, with their funny American-like accents, plenty of chocolate bars and large packets of 'Sweet Caporal Cigarettes' and charming manners. It's no wonder the locals took them to their hearts. We did not know it at the time but I believe that their destination was Dieppe; many did not return. I wish I had understood the dangers they were facing, so that I could have said goodbye properly. One soldier stands out among those we knew, mostly only by their nickname. 'Hank' was a super guy from Ontario, when I visit the War Cemeteries of Northern France, as I often do, I always think of him".

Ted Dyke met his wife-to-be in Bexhill and it was their marriage, on August 15th 1942, at the town's St Peter's Church and his subsequent seven day leave that kept Ted from being part of the Dieppe raid on the 19th, when so many of his comrades died. Of the 4,963 Canadians who participated in the Dieppe Raid, known as Operation Jubilee, 907 were killed, 1,874 taken prisoner and 2,460 wounded. Only 339 of the 2,210 who returned to Britain were unharmed. The Hastings and St Leonards Observer of 22nd August, published a picture on its front page, with the caption: 'The Hastings Lifeboat, The Cyril and Lillian Bishop, was launched on Wednesday, while the combined operation on Dieppe was taking place, it returned to shore with a paravane in tow', there were no further details of the raid. Later, the townspeople were warned to be aware of the possibility of similar raids on Hastings, by German forces.

Peter Longstaff Tyrrell, writer of the Maple Leaf Army in Britain, generously contributed to this book the following, previously unseen letters. With one exception, these Canadian soldiers were never in Hastings but their experiences are probably fairly typical of those who were.

CANADIAN SOLDIER. DAVE HARVARD

"My first posting in England was as reinforcement to the 5th Field Regiment RC Artillery. We lived in tents in Burton Rough, near Petworth in Sussex. We several new recruits were mostly from Western Canada, the province of British Columbia. But most of regiment was from Eastern Canada and they did not welcome us. They were probably reluctant to accept us because of our late (1943) arrival overseas. Most of them had been here since 1940 but we were still in high school then and did not qualify to join up till 1942. We arrived one beautiful summer evening, no effort was made to find us accommodation, so we decided to bed down in a wooded area. Sometime after midnight, we woke to a thunderstorm; there was a deluge of rain and our groundsheets had collected puddles of water. In darkness and completely strange surroundings, we crashed through undergrowth and stinging nettles, to find shelter in a Nissan hut cookhouse, where we passed the rest of the night, soaked through, reclining on the cookhouse concrete floor.

The lovely surrounding countryside and the age of the buildings, particularly Petworth House and those in the village, soon entranced me, but in the autumn we went away on manoeuvres over other parts of England and into Wales. Winter of 1943 found us billeted at Rottingdean, near Brighton, in an unusual wooden building, similar to homes in Canada; we slept on the floors, soldier-style. We were all gunners in that billet and the sergeants used to visit us after 'lights out', to play cards. The NCOs were often unwilling to leave and one night a soldier, wanting to sleep, picked up his Sten gun, loaded it and threatened to shoot out the ceiling light if they did not go. Getting no response, he suited the action to the word. There was no official comeback because the sergeants should not have been there. On a return visit to Rottingdean in 1967, I found that our former billet, at the top of Bazehill Road, had become a guesthouse called 'Seadowns'. When I told the two ladies who owned the guesthouse the story of the lights-out shooting, they said it solved for them the mystery of the holes in the ceiling that were found during renovations.

One incident sticks in my mind: We went on manoeuvres on the downs. En route to Alfriston, we were stopped at a gateway by an old crone, who demanded cigarettes; she got them too, thrown to her gladly. She must have had at least six woollen skirts on, all peppered with holes, she was toothless and her face was deeply creased with blackness. I have fond memories of Rottingdean: Our mess hall was in what must have been a very old house at the bottom of Bazehill Road. We entered the grounds through an arched doorway in a flint stone wall and just inside the house entrance was a piece of stained glass inscribed with the words, 'Merton College'. Could this have been Rudyard Kipling's house? I noted on my last visit to Rottingdean that the price of property was sky high and the place had become a dormitory for London commuters. To me this village is still beautiful, so many fine, old houses and the lovely little village pond. To a young soldier like me, Brighton held many attractions, particularly the ice rink and the dazzling females; these often caused me to miss the last bus and condemned me to the long walk home. On leave in Sussex, I visited my mother's maiden aunt at Old Heathfield. My mother had lived in Eastbourne but my father came from London, both had immigrated to Canada after WWI. My father returned to England as a Canuck to fight in that war. Incidentally, my wife is from Wales, she was a captain in the ATS".

CANADIAN SOLDIER CHARLES BRAZIER. "I was with the 5th Canadian Division Signals from 1941 to 1946. We landed in England in November 1941 and were stationed in Aldershot for 6 months. We then went to Hindhead and from there to a camp called Barton Stacey; we moved on to Crowborough and we stayed at Conan Doyle's former home. I remember this place very well; Conan Doyle was buried in the garden, along with others of his family. We used to go to the village pub and the locals told us the house was haunted. We decided to hold a dance there but we had a hard time to get the local girls to attend; they thought they might see a ghost! From Conan Doyle's House we went to Brighton and were billeted on

Charles Brazier (right) in
Conan Doyle's garden.

Second Street in Hove, near the waterfront. I remember the good times, dancing at the Dome and drinking in Tommy Farr's Bar. From there we went to Eastbourne but we did not stay long, as we were sent over to Italy in November 1943. Both of my parents were born in Fishergate, a suburb of Brighton. They came to Canada in 1912 and raised seven children. My parents used to go back to Brighton after the war for visits".

CANADIAN SOLDIER VICTOR BULGER.

"My regiment, the 1st Regiment Royal Canadian Horse Artillery of the 1st Canadian Division, left Halifax, Canada on the 12th December 1939, and arrived in England around seven days later. On arrival we were stationed at Aldershot. After the British troops were evacuated from Dunkirk on June 4th 1940, the 1st Canadian Brigade, which included my regiment, left Plymouth on 11th June and disembarked at Brest, France, the next day. The brigade moved inland as far as Sable and got within 75 miles of Paris. The next day the Germans took Paris and we were ordered to return to Brest. There, we were told to destroy the vehicles and guns but our C.O. refused to destroy the guns and we quickly loaded them on board the ship, which left Brest on 17th June. We were stationed south of London, around Bromley and Beckenham for the next 15 months. Early in 1941 I was on a light AA Gun site at

Victor Bulger in Florence 1944

Dartford, where there were many war plants. Here, I experienced the air raids on London and witnessed what the British people had to endure; I have tremendous respect for them. I was befriended by a Mr and Mrs Geoff Ruthen, who had a business in Beckenham; they treated me like family. With them, I saw the film Mrs Miniver and I thought that Mrs Ruthen was so like her; in the cheerful and graceful way she looked after her family and her husband's business and kept him supplied with food and coffee, when he was on duty as an Air Raid Warden.

We moved to Arundel, Sussex, near the south coast, in 1941. Our barracks were in an old, cement warehouse, which was heated by small pot-bellied stove in the centre. Arundel is on a hill and around one side of it is the castle. When we were eating in our mess hall, we could look out over the River Arun, with its flock of swans sailing by and see the towers of the castle, the home of the Duke and Duchess of Norfolk; it was an impressive sight. There was a theatre near us and we could go to a two-movie show for 8d (3½ p). Afterwards, we would race to the WVS centre, to get a cup of tea and 3 pieces of toast and jam for 4d (1½ p). Imagine, a night out for a shilling (5p). We could pass an evening in this centre, reading the magazines or playing darts for little or no money. In a nice tearoom, on a side street, they served a huge pot of tea, a large jug of hot water and a fine assortment of cookies. There were also several pubs in the town, which the men frequented in the evenings. Some thirty years later, an old comrade visited one of these pubs and asked the owner if he remembered when the Canadians were stationed there. The owner said he was new to the place and that perhaps some people at the tables would remember them. One lady spoke up 'I certainly remember the b****y Canadians, one of your sergeants made my sister pregnant'. Sometimes it doesn't pay to ask questions! That Christmas, most of us had received parcels from home. We shared the goodies with our comrades and thought of our family back home. The W.V.S. put on a New Year's Dance in Arundel Castle and it was a fine affair.

In the spring of 1942, our battery moved out to Walberton, about 3 miles away, a pleasant little village, with two corner stores and a pub named The Holly Tree. Some evenings, a few of us would walk a couple miles through farmland, to catch a bus to Bognor Regis. The bus driver was a very jovial person and was doing more for the community than just driving. At some stops, a lady might pass him a couple of letters to mail or he would get off and hand mail to someone waiting on the doorstep. At one stop, a lady came out, gave him a cup of tea and chatted for a while, to him and the passengers. Bognor Regis looked almost deserted; tourists were not permitted on the south coast and I think that most of the young people had been called up in the services or to work in munitions factories.

The next month we moved to a few miles south of Lewes; our battery H.Q. was situated in a Farm House called 'Cobbe Place'. The regiment went on several exercises on Lewes Downs, sometimes all night. We slept out around the gun, in the open air. In the morning, our blankets were covered with dew. When the mist lifted, there would be a terrific view of the countryside for miles around. One night, it was Guy Fawkes' and as I was walking back from a movie show, I met a middle-aged lady, going in the same direction. She told me that she was a midwife and had just assisted at the birth of a baby, a short time before. On 29th April 1943, we set off in convoy for Scotland and drove through London with a police escort, going past many of the familiar historical sites, including Trafalgar Square, which was a terrific experience. Our regiment trained in the hills of Scotland until leaving for Sicily in July 1943".

CANADIAN SOLDIER BILL GAYLER
"I was 24 when I arrived in Britain but others were a good bit younger and had never left Canada before. I guess you could say that we adjusted quite well to the climate and the currency and regarded our trip overseas as a 'Great Adventure'. I had joined the Canadian regular army in 1935 at the age of 19, so by 1939, I was quite familiar with military life and was pretty well accustomed to accepting most things as they came along. Most of us found the living conditions in England

to be very similar to our own. We were always received in the friendliest fashion by the English population, wherever we happened to be. As you are no doubt aware, a good percentage of the Canadian population originally came from England or other parts of the British Isles. During our stay in England, in my case, for 3½ years, we were stationed in many locations throughout your country. This varied from a period of several weeks to months at a time. Our last move in England was to Hastings, on 7th August 1942, from West Grinstead, where we had

Bill Gayler in England, 1942.

been under canvas since 1st of May of that year. We spent our last days in England at Hastings, prior to travelling northward to Scotland and then on the Mediterranean and to Sicily".

The air raids on Hastings continued: On the 21st September, two bombs were dropped at 9.25am, which damaged the top story of Marine Court, in use as billets by members of the Royal Air Force; there were no casualties. This was followed on 24th by an attack by seven fighter-bombers with an escort of fighters that dropped bombs on Warrior Square, West Hill, St Leonards, De Cham Road and Quarry Hill, where the home of National Institute for Blind was hit, killing two inmates and injuring several others.

In the autumn of 1942, Hastings Magistrate Court saw its first prosecution under the Misuse of Motor Fuel Rationing Order of 1941. This seems to have been so complicated that it was no wonder that even the most law abiding citizen could quite unintentionally transgress. The law was not entirely clear about what was, 'non-essential purposes', and if you were prudent enough to save up your petrol allowance, then a special licence was required to use it! The hapless offender in the case reported was fined two pounds. The first prosecution was brought against a local citizen, for failing to turn up for fire watching duty. It appeared that the absence was due to a general dissatisfaction with the duty roster and the magistrate decided to take a lenient view, fining the man only two pounds, instead of imposing the harsher prison sentence applicable.

To go along with soap rationing, personal hygiene took another blow, when the government opened the 'Battle for Fuel' in November, with the demand that people should use no more than a five-inch depth of water in their bath and do laundry only once a week. The slogan was 'Save Fuel on the Home Front or Lose Life on the Battle Front' The campaign extended to every aspect of running a home, government posters exhorted: 'Cook several dishes at once. Do not burn ornamental or unnecessary lights. To save coal, put a brick at the back of the grate. Do not put that extra lump of coal on the fire if you are just going to bed. Sift the cinders from the fire, to recover unburned fuel. If every household saves five pounds of coal per day, it will amount to six million tons of coal a year!' Supplies of consumer goods were running low and pleas for householders to donate wireless sets to isolated gun crews and the men on minesweepers brought a poor response. It was rare then for a family to own more than one radio and almost everybody listened to the news several times a day.

Dear Hannah,

For my family, 1942 drew to a close on a very low note. My brother Ron became seriously ill and was confined to bed in a darkened room. He was far too sick to give any attention to me and he grew steadily worse, often lapsing into delirium; just after Christmas, he was taken into Farnborough Hospital. After the ambulance had gone I went to his empty room and looked at the impression of his head in the pillow and wondered if he would come back to us. My mother was devastated and, although still working, she would make the long journey by bus to visit Ron in hospital. She journeyed back through heavy, night-time air raids and often arrived home trembling and in tears. I recall that I went to an amateur pantomime, put on in a village or church hall. It was the first stage show I had ever seen but my main thought was, how can people be laughing and clapping, when my dear brother may be dying? It was a wretched Christmas.

With Very Much Love, Gran'ma.

1942

In Hastings, the seafront curfew was relaxed for the three-day Christmas period, from 10:15pm to1:00am. On Christmas Day, church bells were rung, a practice that had ceased since it had become a warning of enemy invasion. American troops gave a party at their camp for the children of an outlying village, using lorries to collect all the children aged between two and sixteen. The youngsters enjoyed entertainment and played American games, ate doughnuts and peanuts and drank coca cola; one soldier had made a huge box of chocolate fudge. The children were given funds for a treat and each went home with an armful of goodies. The final edition of the 1942 Hastings and St Leonards Observer carried a two-page tribute to the town's war effort on the Home Front, which praised its 'Courage, Humour and Spirit.' It came as no surprise to see how many of the articles and photographs featured women.

1943

National economic statistics published early in 1943 revealed that over the previous 12 months, Britain has reduced its annual consumption to four fifths, although incomes had risen by 50% since 1938. Rationing, shortages and high taxation affected family life and less money had been spent on food, clothing and travel but expenditure on alcohol and tobacco had doubled. Many items were manufactured to utility standards and some everyday requirements, such as razor blades, torch batteries, pens and pencils were only available to favoured customers, 'under the counter'. Every means of reducing needless production was pursued; the government said that in order to save on dye, only standard grey or blue school uniforms would be allowed.

Dear Hannah,
My brother stayed in Farnborough Hospital for months, his original illness was diagnosed as a mastoid infection, which was followed by meningitis. It was the new drug, penicillin that saved his life. He then suffered a paralysis, which the doctor thought was polio. He lost the use of his voice and both arms, which had to be fixed above his head, in splints. His bed was in one of the hospital's asbestos-roofed huts, set up in the grounds, as temporary wards for wounded First World War Soldiers. I was not permitted to go to his bedside, so I looked at him through a window, miming jokes, in a sad attempt to revive our jollier times together. The heavy night raids were terrifying for him. It was not possible to move him, so when all the other patients were taken to the air raid shelters he had to remain behind, in what was not much more than a shed. The ward sister, an intimidating woman with a glass eye, volunteered to stay with Ron. She sat by his bed, wearing a tin hat, while the flashes of bomb explosions and gunfire reflected eerily in her prosthetic eye. My brother was very nervous of her at the time but now pays tribute to her great courage.

Exhibit of wartime family in museum, Chislehurst caves.
Source: Helen Edith Stephenson.

97

At home, my mother and I had lived through the terrible night raids, when the skies above our house were rent with hours of deafening gunfire. We had no air raid shelter so remained in bed and one night, we saw, through the uncurtained window, a German plane explode in a fireball, in mid-air. We clasped each other and wept in terror, gabbling prayers, pleading to God for our survival. After this, my mother and I started to go to the Chislehurst Caves, which were used as air raid shelters by thousands of people from London. I hated the caves, the tunnels were filled with wooden bunk beds and being a child I was expected to sleep at the top, with my face inches from the chalk walls and roof of the cave, it was like being buried alive. During the night the caverns echoed with the snores, coughs and groans of thousands of sleepers. I recently discovered that at one time during the war, the shelter users numbered up to 15,000. The whole set up was very well organised, with a chapel, hospital, canteen and entertainments, and a set of rules, with 'Cave Captains' to enforce them. Chislehurst Caves are now a visitor attraction, with wax figures installed to represent the WWII cave dwellers.

You many well ask, where was my father when my mother and I were having these experiences? I have only just learned the answer; he did not accompany us to the caves because he spent the nights sitting in a shelter, close to Farnborough Hospital gates, in case his son needed assistance in an air raid. How I wish I had known that at the time.

With Very Much Love, Gran'ma.

The heaviest air raid attacks on Hastings occurred during 1943. Early in January, an enemy plane was brought down, as it attempted to cross the channel. It hit an unoccupied bungalow and burst into flames, killing the crew. Wreckage was strewn over a radius of fifty yards. Local fire parties tried to douse the petrol flames, amid exploding cannon shells; the National Fire Service finally brought the blaze under control. The only part of the plane that had remained intact was the tail. Early one afternoon, in the same period, two enemy planes, with guns blazing, swooped on a field where three Land Army girls were working. The girls took shelter in a shed; the bullets killed a pony and seriously injured two cows. AA guns brought one raider down.

Monica , aged 14½, set off on her way to a new life: "It was a daunting journey for me, alone, with just written instructions, as all destination markings and signposts had been removed, to confuse enemy invaders. I set forth, regarding it as a bit of an adventure. I must have looked a sight, in my old coat and poke bonnet, carrying the little attaché case my sister had used for her schoolwork; it easily held the very few items of clothing I possessed. My uncle met me at Victoria Station and we caught a bus to his house in Barnes; I was very impressed with his knowledge of London but he had lived there most of his life. It also struck me how smart and pretty the girls in town looked. On the Monday morning, Uncle took me to the office of his friend, my new 'Boss' and I returned to his farm with him. I was glad to see my brother again and I enjoyed my first meal on the farm. I was awakened on the next morning by the 'Boss', with a cup of tea and told to get up and put on a brown overall coat and the Wellington boots I would find downstairs and go out to the cowshed. I was somewhat apprehensive, never before having been very close to a cow.

In April 1943, my brother left the farm, as he was so unhappy and he found employment in an aircraft factory in the nearest town. This was until he became 17 and able to join the navy. I was left alone, to attend the cows and then I had to go back to the house, with the daily milk supply. After breakfast I would do housework, making the beds and tidying the six bedrooms and two bathrooms. Then I went back to the dairy to sterilise the milking machines and join in the many and varied jobs on the farm. I loved the animals dearly but there were some jobs I didn't like; I can remember picking sprouts in January till my hands froze and I was glad when warmer days came. During one summer evening, when making the last drinks of the day for visitors, I was amazed to overhear myself being talked about and being referred to as 'abused'. They also called me a child, which made me feel indignant, as I felt very grown up, doing an adult's job and taking on all sorts of responsibilities. Someone must have contacted my uncle because at the end of that year, as suddenly as he decided to send me there, he made me leave, just before Christmas. I went back to my stepmother but she was unable to re-accommodate me, so the owner of the village shop allowed me to stay with my sister, in her room over the shop".

1943

Dear Hannah,

The brother Monica talks about in her WWII experiences is your grandfather. I met him in 1950; he was recently out of the navy and on a government, agricultural scheme for ex-serviceman. I was a schoolgirl, living on the farm where he came to train and work. He valued his time in naval service but rarely spoke of his wartime

Hannah's paternal grandfather,
aged 13 years.

experiences. I know from the few things he said that he had some terrible war experiences. Long after the war he continued to suffer from what is now called post-traumatic stress disorder and I feel it may have been a contributory factor to his premature death. I love this photo of him in his Sea Scout uniform. At the age of 13 he had been in the Hastings Sea Scout Company that met at the St Leonards Bathing Pool.

When my brother Derrick joined the navy he trained at HMS Collingwood and was then assigned to the destroyer, HMS Matchless. He went on many Russian convoys, including to Murmansk. During one of these, in December 1943, the Matchless was involved in action with the German Battleship, Sharnhorst, which was sunk. Of the Sharnhorst's complement of nearly 2,000 men only 36 were hauled from the freezing waters. I have recently read, Her Name Was Matchless, written by one of Derrick's shipmates, Richard Gordon

Butler. From this book I have learned something of the hardships and terrors faced by my brother at sea in WWII. No wonder he just wanted to booze, go wild and then sleep when he was on leave. Later in the war, he applied to become a deep-sea diver, the medical tests were very rigorous and although in magnificent health, he failed because his ears bled when he went beyond a certain depth, so he became a torpedo man, on the submarine, HMS Universal. He is almost 80 years old now and with his ruddy face and profuse, curly grey hair and beard he looks the very image of an old sea dog!

It was in 1943 that my Canadian cousins, Albert and Bob, arrived in Great Britain with their regiment. My father had 10 sisters and brothers, two of his brothers emigrated, one to Australia, the other to Canada. Family legend has it that the brother who went to Canada took as a bride a North American Native, who he had freed from her bond slavery to a farmer. The appearance of her eldest son, Albert, may have evidenced this. He was big, taciturn and swarthy and spoke very little, so different from his brother Bob, who was like my father, small, talkative and mercurial. Their arrival in my life brought an element of excitement. They gave us supplies of food and I experienced a feeling of wealth when I saw the tinned goods and chocolate in the kitchen cupboard. I was entranced by my Canadian cousins' accents, indistinguishable to me from that of American film stars, and by their confidence and good-natured generosity. Neighbours' teenaged daughters were also very smitten! This cousin-exchange worked both ways. My brother Derrick went to Australia with the Royal Navy in 1944 and was able to visit his father's brother and family on several occasions.

With Very Much Love, Gran'ma.

Tuesday, 9th February, was a morning of heavy cloud and rain in Hastings, when two German bombers took advantage of the poor visibility to carry out a raid. Miss Christine Hayward, then aged 7, the child of the green grocer at Ore Village, remembers the raid well: "We had beds in the cellars underneath the shop and we had been sleeping there during the worst of the raids. I was not at school on the day of the attack, as I had a cold and the weather was so bad. A man who was delivering vegetables to us at 10.00am saw incendiary bombs falling and he rushed in, shouting to us to take cover and we all ran under the stairs, just as bombs struck. I can't remember the noise but it must have been loud. My mother said later that something had told her not to go into the cellar for shelter and as it turned out, the dividing wall of the cellar collapsed on the place where we usually went. We might have been killed or injured had we gone there. None of us were hurt but all the windows were blown out and the shop was on fire. The neighbours helped us put it out because the fire brigade was so busy elsewhere. The bomb blast had sent my dad's outside display of fruit and vegetables over the roof of the Hare and Hounds, the pub on the other side of the road, and into its backyard. Our shop front, the bedroom above it and my bed were blown to bits. Dad then rented a house in nearby Edmund Road and we lived there for a year, until our house and shop were repaired. A few days after the raid, Dad opened up a shop along the road from ours. The Mayor of Hastings sent him a letter of thanks for this. Four years later, we still used to dig up pieces of my mother's jewellery from our garden".

During this raid, bombs had fallen right across the borough, from Ore

Mr Hayward's bombed shop, Ore Village.
Source: Christine Hayward.

to Hollington, demolishing one church and damaging another; three people were killed and five injured three of them seriously. A Hastings to London train was strafed by enemy cannon fire and Driver Robert Willey made for the shelter of a tunnel at top speed. The train took a few bullets but nobody was hurt. This was not the first experience of its kind for Mr Willey; another train he was driving was machine-gunned, as it crossed the marshes. Even nature conspired; the week before these raids, the town had suffered considerably from the effect of gales that damaged roofs and the already derelict St Leonards Pier.

As if to recompense the population, an exhibition of 50 photographs was mounted at Woolworth, showing the destructive effect of RAF bombing on Germany and enemy occupied territory. In spite of the terrors and emergencies of war, the town tried to continue its normal life. A special luncheon was planned to commemorate the 25th anniversary of the granting of the Royal Assent to the first Women's Suffrage Measure. It revived memories of the early days of the Votes for Women Movement, when Mrs Pankhurst addressed an open-air meeting in Hastings. In the First World War the Women's Suffrage Movement suspended its activities for the duration of hostilities. An early, local supporter, Miss Tristram, one of the guests at the forthcoming lunch, was employed as the only woman on a WWI recruiting committee. How things change; by 1943, there were 67,000 members of the Women's Voluntary Service active in the South East Region. In Hastings, they added to their more serious duties the task of teaching soldiers to darn socks and patch clothing. The local paper reported that the soldiers encountered the same problems as children do on learning to sew; the difficulty in threading needles and the mistake of using too long a thread, accompanied in this case by very unchildlike language!

Food problems on the home front increased; dried milk was introduced, under the name 'Household Milk'; this was on points and the allocation was one tin per ration book per month. In a bleak advert, biscuit manufacturers, McVite and Price, posed the question, 'Are biscuits really necessary?' and added, 'At such times, the Forces must have them, as they are a sustaining and nourishing food, ready to hand'. In other words, biscuits for civilian consumption were in short supply. The nation was urged yet again, by the Potato Publicity Board, to eat more potatoes and less bread, to preserve grain stocks and cut down on the use of shipping. Hastings, in common with the rest of the country, had Potato Week. The local newspaper offered a prize for the best potato recipe, and another for the shop with the best window display of British grown produce. Miss Potter, of 43, Ashburnham Road, won 42/- (£2.20) and a sack of potatoes for her recipe for a bacon roll, which incorporated dried egg, sage and onion stuffing, a small amount of bacon and, of course, potatoes. Pont's, in Queens Avenue, still a greengrocer today, were awarded the five-pound prize for the best-dressed window.

I'm an Energy Food! Says 'POTATO PETE'

1943

A Wings for Victory Week was announced for the coming mid-May and Hastings was told it must aim for a total of £300,000. The country as a whole was given a target of £150 million. Hastings' 'Patriotic Batchelor', who had offered a gift of a National Savings Certificate to every child born in the 1941 War Weapons Week, extended the same offer for Wings for Victory Week. Young William Winston White, nearly two and one of the earlier recipients of the newborn's National Saving Certificate award, was pictured in the local paper, at the door of his home in the Old Town, with National Savings Collector, Miss Potter. (She of the bacon roll fame, perhaps?) Hastings had 259 savings groups and the town's total war savings from January 1940 to January 1943 amounted to over three million pounds.

Hastings was promised a new air raid warning system, to be installed by August, to give an instant warning of when enemy aircraft were in the immediate vicinity. An adapter, fitted to the standard siren, would enable it to make a fractured or 'cuckoo' sound, very distinct from the normal, undulating wail. Long before this could be put in place, the town suffered a terrible attack on the afternoon of Thursday 11th March. Joyce Brewer remembers, "I had just got in from doing my milk round and was eating my dinner, when all hell broke loose. I rushed to the door to see our street's gun firing, with the barrel dropped to its lowest angle, pointing at the planes that were skimming over Alexandra Park and Blacklands Church. The enemy planes came in very low, in groups of twenty five, ME109s and FW 190s, dropping larger bombs and leaving before our RAF boys arrived."

War Weapons Week Baby Is Still Saving

Miss Potter collects Old Town National Savings
Source: HSLO

Hastings naval man Ray Gladwish, who served on the Minesweeper, HMS Speedwell, recalls being on leave during March 1943, when Silverhill Junction and many other parts of the town suffered during this attack. Ray was visiting some friends near Silverhill at the time

Ray Gladwish aboard the Minesweeper 'Speedwell'

and he ran to the bombed houses, to help the rescuers. He recalls digging out a woman, who had her child clasped in her arms; both were dead. Her weeping husband sat among the ruins. Ray said: "I was used to seeing injury and death at sea, we all had to accept it as part of war but it was so much more terrible to me when civilians were involved and it was almost a relief to go back off leave".

Frank Strudwick, who was only five years old in 1943 said, "My family has very vivid memories of the 11th March raid, when we had the back of our house blown in, by the bomb that flattened houses in Salisbury Road. The street formed a square, along with Horntye Road, Cranbrook Road and St. Paul's Road, the back gardens were all adjoining. We lived in St. Paul's Road, about 100 yards away from the spot where the bomb fell and our house caught the full blast. My father and brother were in bed with some illness, and my sister had just got home from school. Dad shouted to her and she had the sense to get under the Morrison Shelter. My brother tells me that my father had to lift the wardrobe doors from his bed, as they had been torn off by the blast. Then it took him about 15 minutes to reach my sister because he was blinded by dust and all the house's interior doors had been blown inside out. While all this was happening, I was on the seafront with my mother, as enemy aircraft were firing tracer bullets into the old St.Leonards pier. I can clearly remember looking out from under her, as she lay on me, and telling her that they were fireworks. She told me later that she kept repeating to herself: 'I'm still alive, I'm still alive', almost as if the words would keep her alive. One of the houses near ours that was destroyed was the home of a neighbouring family named Wareham; Mrs Wareham and her twenty-four year old daughter were killed. My brother was friendly with her son, Colin, who survived, as did his father, brother and other sister. Because I was only 5 at the time, the tragedy didn't register with me and I remember getting excited when I found odd cigarette cards and marbles on the bombsite, when all the rubble was cleared". During this horrific raid, shops at Silverhill and many houses throughout the town were demolished. St Matthews School, providentially empty, was wrecked and two hospitals were blast damaged. In all, 38 people were killed, 39 seriously injured and 51 slightly injured. The Duchess of Kent made a surprise visit to the town almost immediately after the raid. She inspected the Civil Defence and post air raid services and the St Clements Caves' shelters. The Duchess was dressed in black, still in deep mourning for her husband, The Duke of Kent, who had been killed in a mystery air crash, in August 1942.

Hastings Corporation continued to chew over the matter of bus queue regulations and solved the problem at York Buildings by erecting railings, with exits, where the buses pulled up. Councillor Riddle said this system would, 'frustrate the sneaks, who dodge from one queue to another'. This preoccupation with what may seem a petty matter reflected the transport situation; there were almost no private cars, so public transport was much in demand and it was not unusual for some of the queue to be left behind, due to lack of room in the bus. The new system was so successful it was extended to other bus stops in the town. Shortages of everyday commodities and services had turned queuing everywhere into a daily exercise and most British people strictly observed queue etiquette; queue jumpers were soon put in their place, in both senses!

For Easter Sunday, 1943, the War Cabinet announced that existing regulations concerning the invasion warning could be relaxed and church bells were rung. In the light of changing circumstances, the coastal ban was lifted for the first time for three years but there was no semblance of a rush to the seaside, with the Good Friday being the quietest holiday on record. Hastings people opted for a stay at home holiday, tending gardens and allotments and enjoying local facilities. Hastings had coffee and evening dances, the cinemas did good business, as did the larger of the two White Rock Swimming Baths, specially opened for the holiday. The fund raising events for Wings for Victory Week had been underway some days before its 15th May start, when the town was told that the original target of £300,000 was to be raised to £400,000. In addition to the usual fundraisers; socials, concerts, dances and sports events, the Red Cross was selling special stamps in the foyer of the Ritz Cinema. These were stuck all over a 500-pound, bomb until it was completely covered. Mid-week there was parade of troops and local civil defence organisations, with the Hastings Mayor taking the salute at the town hall. On Saturday 22nd May, the local paper announced that the target for the Wings for Victory Week was raised to half million pounds, the equivalent of 100 fighter aircraft.

A new law had just come into force, aimed at supposed women 'shirkers' and the Ministry of Labour had the power to direct those between 18 and 45 into compulsory, part-time war work. Mothers caring for children under 14 years old were exempt. Caring for the children of working women was also regarded as a form of war work. At that time, there were 600,000 female part-time workers but more were needed. Women made up 57% of the workforce of ordnance factories and 40% of the engineering industry. Nine out of ten single women and eight out of ten married women were in industry or the auxiliary forces. By the end of July, the Minister of Labour, Ernest Bevin had stopped recruitment into the women's uniformed services, to divert more women and girls of 16 and 17 into aircraft production. There were to be no more volunteers accepted into the ATS, WAAF, WRENS and the Women's Land Army. The labour force was still insufficient and women of up to aged 50 were to be registered for war work. By September 1943,

If *you* can't go to the factory help the neighbour who *can*

CARING FOR WAR WORKERS' CHILDREN IS A NATIONAL SERVICE

Britain was almost totally mobilized; 70% of the 33 million women and men between ages 16 to 64 were in the armed forces, civil defence or some form of war work. One million people aged over 65 were also in employment. Around 100,000 women had joined the railways and some were working as welders in shipyards. Even then, the Ministry of Labour predicted a forthcoming manpower crisis. Inevitably, the change in the status of women, the absence of men from home and the perils and uncertainties of war impinged on family life and influenced moral attitudes.

By the spring of 1943 David Evans' days as a Bexhill teenage Home Guard were far behind him, he was in Terrell, Texas, with the RAF, on a flying course. He travelled across Canada to Detroit and in a letter to his parents dated 1st April he wrote of his journey and experiences:

My Dear Mum and Dad,

I am now 5,000 miles from home and the only way I can send mail is by the long route; overland by rail and then by sea to England. We had the heck of a long rail journey in Canada and were in Monkton for a short while. Before we had got over the awful sea journey, we were off again, on trains. The scenery became more beautiful as we progressed; we spent the nights sleeping across two train seats. We arrived at Detroit and then in the morning we ran into Chicago and we were disappointed not to see any bank robberies in progress! We had a half hour stop at St Louis; here we were pounced on by Americans, who showered us with hospitality. Throughout our journey we ate in the dining car, very excellent meals with ice cream included. We continued our rail journey and the following morning we woke up in Texas; the fresh grass and trees here remind me of an English spring.

We are very comfortable here, the food is so perfect I feel as though it is peacetime; we always have ice cream for the fourth course for dinner and tea. For every meal we can have as much milk as we want, I always have at least half a pint at each meal. We get pretty good sleeping hours in; our beds have lovely soft mattresses, set on large springs. I expected the usual RAF 'boards' when I jumped into bed and I was flung about 10 feet into the air! The spring weather is very hot and can be tiresome but we have hot weather clothing and eating an orange now and then keeps you cool. I certainly wish you were here to have some of this food.

I met a Bexhill boy today, whom I knew at school and we had a good old pow-wow. I remember him from when we had a boxing bout in the school tournament. The Terrell people are extremely kind to us, last night I was invited to a party in the town, where we were immediately made to feel at home. We are only 30 miles from Dallas and apparently the people there wait your arrival and invite you to their houses for the weekend. We have done some flying but I encountered my old trouble of airsickness today, while doing stalls and spins. I felt bad, I wasn't actually sick but I'll get used to it.

I have already sent a cable to you with my address. Will you just keep writing to me because all these letters take a very long time? I can only send a cable every so often because 24 words cost about 11/- (55p) in our money. So cheerio for a while, you folks.

Tons of love from your affectionate son,
David

The story of David's posting to America appeared in the Bexhill-on-Sea Observer. The newspaper printed another of his letters to his parents, written during a seven-day leave. He described his travels and once again the kindness and open-heartedness of the American people: 'The uniform draws a crowd and I am pleased to find that the Royal Air Force ranks high in people's estimation here. The Americans are wonderful and I won't listen to a bad word that anyone might say about them. Churchill always gets heavy applause when he is on the news in cinema shows and it does my heart good to see how popular he is over here. The Americans are enormously patriotic and they are keen to show it but they are impressed by our quiet patriotism. They love their flag and country and are most keen to get on the friendliest terms with Great Britain. They tell me how much they marvelled at the British courage during the Battle of Britain, which makes me feel proud to be in the RAF. I am hoping to go to a dance in Houston tonight. I rather enjoy the American's way of dancing because it is a case of dancing just what you like, with complete disregard for the timing of the music'.

Dear Hannah,

Compare David Evan's account of a British serviceman in the USA with the story of an American soldier, stationed in England, taking leaves in London in 1944. The hospitality of the British people is not lacking, just the practical means to express it. It's gratifying that Bob Gallagher, the former GI who wrote the following piece, was aware of the sacrifice the English family made to provide him and his friends with as good a meal as they were able.

I have been unable to find an American soldier who was stationed in or near Hastings in WWII but, as with the Canadians, I think we can take Bob's account as typical. My view of Americans today is coloured by my encounters with the few I met in my wartime childhood. For whatever reasons, they helped us in a time of terrible trouble and I will never forget that.

With very much love Gran'ma

Bob Gallagher wrote: 'Sometime in January, I got a four-day pass and went to London with two of my buddies. We had a wonderful time. We stayed in a private home near Marble Arch, in the area known as the West End. We saw all the sights, night and day. Most of the bomb damage in London was in the East End. Where we were staying there were only a few buildings damaged but one evening, when I had just gone to bed, the explosion of German rocket nearby, also called a "Buzz Bomb", awakened me. I heard a lot of sirens, but I never saw the damage where it hit.

London had a lot of clubs and places to go for the GIs, including some with dancing. We would also go to the movies there. When the movie was over, we had to stand at attention while they played the British National Anthem. We would always try and cut out early but the projectionist would start it before the last words were said. Despite the tight blackout restrictions, there was an active nightlife going on in London. My friends and I were still having a problem adapting to the beer that was served at room temperature, so our trips to the pubs were held to a minimum. One of the things we would do, in addition to sightseeing, was to go over to the entrance to Hyde Park, near Marble Arch, and heckle the soapbox orators. We would harass them verbally and shake the little stands they were on. The Bobbies would come over and politely tell us to stop.

Bob Gallagher (extreme left) with buddies.

While I was in London on this trip, I wanted to get a good meal at a first class restaurant. I knew that England had price restrictions on everything, including food in restaurants, so I wasn't too concerned about the price. My comrades and I picked out a very fancy looking place in the better part of town, which still had a doorman, even though he was probably in his eighties. We went in and ordered one of the more expensive entrees on the menu. What we wanted was a good steak. We did not realize that there was no such thing on the menus in England. What we ordered, however, sounded like a good cut of beef. What we got was anything but that. The meat was a small roll that might be called a meat loaf except it was so loaded down with bread and other fillers that it wasn't even a meat colour. It came with a large dry baked potato, plain carrots and cabbage. The portions were large and tasteless. The three of us were struggling to get it down. There was a shortage of waiters so we could not even get refills of our tiny water glasses to help wash the food down. There were several large posters scattered around the restaurant that stated, in effect, that the King doesn't waste food so you shouldn't either.

About a month after the first furlough, I got another three-day pass to London. The English people treated us with the greatest kindness. They could not do enough for the GI's. One of my buddies had distant relatives in London, and we went to see them and they invited us for dinner. Even though they had strict rationing for all of their food, they wanted to share it with us. The family consisted of a husband, a wife, and two young children. The main course was a rump roast that weighed about two pounds. We each got two small slices of it. We filled up on potatoes and cabbage - their main staples. After the meal, they told us that the roast was the family ration of meat for the month. We offered them cigarettes, but they refused, so we left some without them knowing about it. Cigarettes were a real luxury, and in some ways, they were better than money. In those days almost everyone smoked, especially in England and Europe. There was no black market in England; at least none that I saw. The people took the war very seriously, and they seemed to put the 'war effort', as they called it, before their own needs. They had a very tough time of it for many years, and yet their spirits always seemed to be high".

As the Wings for Victory week closed, on 23rd May, Hastings suffered a devastating Sunday lunchtime raid, which inflicted death, injury and destruction in a matter of a few minutes. The raid began at one minute to one, carried out by German fighter-bombers that came in underneath cloud, from the east side of the town. They flew low along the seafront, dropping bombs and machine gunning. Five public houses, full of customers were hit, as well as shops and hotels. First

Bomb ruins of Reeves Antiques. Source: HSLO

aid volunteer Noel Care was off duty, having lunch at home; He said, of the bombing and its aftermath: "I was halfway through my meal, when I was called on duty. First of all we went to Reeves Antique Shop in the Old Town High Street. It had collapsed into the road but luckily it was unoccupied and we dealt with a few slight casualties, mostly injuries from flying glass. We were ordered to move on further down the street but it was blocked by the bomb debris of buildings, including the Swan Inn, under which many people were buried. A rescue party was hard at work and we helped the first aid people, already on the spot, treating the casualties as they were pulled out. We were then ordered to move on to the rear of Marine Court, where two women, who had been walking on the cliff top, were half buried in soil and rubble at the foot of the cliffs. We found that one woman had been decapitated; the other was unconscious and had suffered multiple fractures. Marine Court had structural damage but there were no casualties. We still had no idea of the extent of the effects of the raid and imagined we would go off duty at that point. However, we were sent to the Queen's Hotel, which, along with the adjoining Albany Hotel had been taken over for accommodation by the armed services;

Collapsed Albany Hotel.
Source: HSLO

1943

Bob Thornely, Hastings WWII fireman.

the Albany was home to the Royal Canadian Hussars. A freak incident had wrought havoc. A bomb had entered a window of the Queens Hotel, slid along a table, exited through a wall and hit the Albany Hotel. Fortunately, because it was Sunday, most of the soldiers were out of the buildings. When we arrived at the wrecked Albany Hotel, it was agreed by the army authorities that the civilian emergency services could assist on what was technically military property. The uninjured troops had gallantly tried to carry out rescue work themselves, but they had no experience of dealing with demolished buildings. Many of them were suffering from severe cuts to hands and arms, sustained during their frantic efforts to find their comrades. I had to leave the site in the evening, but the work to clear the bomb sites of the Albany and Swan Hotel went on for several days". During this raid the Warrior Gate Hotel, on the corner of Norman Road and London Road, St. Leonards, suffered a direct hit and then caught fire.

Bob Thornely, proprietor of the Ashburnham Dairies, at Mount Road, Hastings, was out delivering milk that Sunday lunchtime, with his son Ivor, aged six. He often went on the milk delivery round with his father, in a Raleigh three-wheeler. Bob Thornely was exempt from military service, as he was in essential employment but he fulfilled wartime duty by joining the Auxiliary Fire Service and later the National Fire Service. Throughout the war, Hastings and St Leonards had a number of emergency fire stations and Bob delivered milk to all of these. As Ivor recalls, these stations were at Priory Road Halton, Mount Road, Clive Avenue, Shepherd Street, Seaside Road, Moreton House, Silverhill Junction Corporation Yard and the 18th century stables, at the High Street entrance to the Old Town.

Just before one o'clock, Bob and young Ivor were going down the hill to the stables when the siren went. They noticed that the guns on the cliffs at High Wickham were being rotated, to point out to sea and they immediately opened fire. Bob stopped the van at the top of the High Street and he and Ivor lay down in the gutter. They heard two huge explosions, as bombs destroyed the Swan Inn, Reeves' antique shop and damaged other buildings in the Old Town. In this raid, Ivor's little friend, Ann Christine Tester, aged 6, who lived at 55, Belmont Road, was killed as she sat on the doorstep of the Swan Inn. Later on the same day, Bob

Marie Gale, aged 3 years

Thornley attended the fire, with the NFS, at the Warrior Gate Hotel and three of his comrades almost lost their lives, when the entire wall of the hotel collapsed. The first aid at the scene of fires was fairly basic and Ivor remembers seeing his father return home with his bloody and injured hands merely swathed in wrappings of mutton cloth waste. Bob had escaped injury or death on his milk round on another occasion, when he was crossing a railway bridge at the back of West St Leonards Station and an enemy plane started machine-gunning the lines.

Because of the war emergency, Ivor Thornely had no formal education until the age of seven, when he attended the Clive Vale School. He recalls that the school's dining room was turned into an air raid shelter, with bricked up windows and sandbagged walls. Like most children, Ivor took the war in his stride. His ambition was to be a road sweeper and he had a little broom and an old doll's pram to help him play out his dream. When the siren went, he would go into anybody's home or air raid shelter for protection, not unusual behaviour during the war. When his parents went to look for him they would spot his 'barrow' and brush, abandoned on the pavement outside the place where he was sheltering. Ivor did not become a road sweeper but a general engineer and he helped in the conversion work on one of his father's milk delivery points, the old stables, which is now a flourishing theatre and art gallery.

Marie Gale, who lived in Hardwicke Road, which overlooks the Old

Town, has strong childhood memories of the 23rd May raid. "My two aunts had taken me for the customary Sunday morning walk and we were on our way home from the Fishmarket and going up the High Street, when the younger aunt wanted to go into the Swan Inn for a drink. There was a little girl sitting on the doorstep and it was suggested I could sit with her. My other aunt said we should press on, as gran would be getting the Sunday lunch, so we continued up the hill, when the dreaded siren went off. My aunts wanted to lay in the gutter, but I refused because I was wearing a new dress my mother had made from parachute 'silk' and I thought she would be cross if I got it dirty. I remember running up Croft Road, in fact my aunts dragged me, to find somewhere to take cover. We eventually went into a house at the top of Salter's Lane, where we were pushed under the stairs. I could see out of a window and I saw a bomb fall, followed by the explosion that demolished the Swan Inn. I eventually went to school with the younger sister of the little girl who was killed on the Swan Inn doorstep".

Also on 23rd May, the cellar of the Tower Hotel was penetrated by a bomb, which did not explode. A bomb disposal squad subsequently removed it. This story had an interesting sequel 47 years on, when a Peter Kavenagh of Coventry, wrote to the Hastings Observer in 1990. He said: 'I was a member of the bomb disposal squad that cleared a bomb from a pub in Hastings in WWII. I knew that a chap from the local newspaper took a photo of the event and I bought the paper for weeks after, but the picture was not published. On later investigation I discovered that had it been published during the war, the editor could have been sentenced to life imprisonment. Many years later, I was visiting my daughter, who lives in Hastings and I took a stroll to the nearest pub. I got chatting to a customer and was telling him about the incident of the unexploded bomb, saying I could not remember the name of the pub. He drew my attention to a photograph behind the bar and it was the one I had seen taken all those years ago and here I was, sitting in The Tower, the very pub from which we had removed the bomb! I was delighted to see the picture, it brought back memories of brave men, some of whom did not survive the war and of the old ones who are left'.

The edition of the Hastings and St Leonards Observer following the

23rd May raid carried a front-page montage of pictures of the town's bomb-wrecked buildings. Only one person and a dog had been rescued alive from the Swan Hotel, the bodies of the licensee's wife and three year old child was not recovered until the following day. Eleven Canadian soldiers were killed in the Albany Hotel. During the raid, a total of 25 people were killed, 30 seriously injured and 55 slightly injured. Days later, in one of those bizarre outcomes of bombing, a canary was dug out alive from the ruins of a house. It was found trapped in a cage that was flattened to a height of about two inches. The rescue workers said the bird was, 'soon hopping about and chirping cheerfully'. The local newspaper made a low-key announcement that the total sum raised during Wings for Victory Week was £521,270,000. A month after the 23rd May air raid attack, a man was sentenced to three months hard labour for looting drinking glasses and a clock from the bomb ruins of a local, un-named hotel.

Dear Hannah,

The spot where the Swan Inn stood is now a garden of remembrance. I sit there sometimes and watch groups of school children and overseas students stop and read the plaque that commemorates the raid and loss

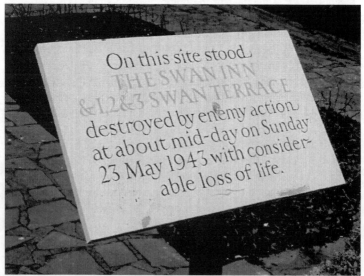

The Swan Inn Garden memorial plaque. Source: Adam Allchin.

of life. How long ago it must seem to these youngsters. Marie Gale told me she thinks of that dreadful morning every time she passes Swan Gardens. By a curious irony, just across the road from the gardens, is a WWII memorabilia and collectibles shop, called 'Don't Mention the War'. Its tiny interior is crammed with gasmasks, uniforms, wartime books, leaflets and documents, the equipment of war, spent ammunition, bayonets and guns.

Although recent television pictures of Iraqi children playing with abandoned weapons were shocking, they did not surprise me. Children will turn anything into a source of interest and fun and wartime Chislehurst was soon providing a variety of new play places for our gang, in the shape of bombed houses and their gardens. I don't know if children still play house but it was a great favourite in my childhood and here were ready-made 'dens', where we could set up home. We were too young to comprehend the tragedy behind the wreckage of these family homes and once inside the girls would set about re-creating a domestic scene among the ruins, while the boys ran riot. In the bedroom of a large bombed house near Chislehurst Common, the boys built a contraption from chunks of brickwork and lengths of floorboard. It became a wobbly springboard, from which they would fling themselves into a roof hatch, set in the bedroom's upper wall. I tried it just once and I recall the terror, followed by exhilaration, as I tumbled, unscathed, in the roof space. I looked out between shattered slates and rafters to the garden below, with its neglected grass, vegetables, fruit trees and bushes. We would usually eat whatever produce we could find in the bombed house gardens; this was scrumping par excellence!

The war had also provided another inviting 'playhouse', the garden Anderson Shelter. Householders put considerable effort into making these attractive and homely; their earth covered tops became flower gardens or for the more practical, a good place to grow vegetable marrows. Their unwelcoming interiors were fitted out with duckboards, to protect feet from the cold earth and sometimes, floodwater. Bunk beds were installed and other little comforts introduced, to ease the misery of being enclosed in what was a tin box in the ground. The public underground shelters were unattractive play places; they often smelled bad, as passersby sometimes used the entrances as lavatories and this, along with their pitch darkness,

discouraged us. We also believed they were haunted and any child
venturing deep inside one alone would win considerable admiration.

With Very Much Love, Gran'ma.

In Hastings in early July 1943, Dominion Day was marked with
particular solemnity, by an open-air ceremony at Heroes' Corner in the
Borough Cemetery; the service was arranged by the town's Canadian
Ex-Servicemen's Organisation. The twenty assembled units of various
local voluntary units made an impressive site and the British Liaison
Officer, Captain Ackroyd, paid tribute to the Canadian Army in Britain
saying: 'They have been a tower of strength to us during the threat of
invasion during 1940 and 1941'. As the tide of war turned, a mood of
hope began to colour expectations and attitudes. Hastings Corporation
opened discussion of a number of schemes for the post-war future of
the town and whether its main potential was as a holiday resort or
residential community. The government announced that signposts
could be re-erected in rural areas, as it seemed the danger of invasion
had receded. Tank traps, anti-tank trenches and barbed wire
entanglements were also removed from where they were considered to
be no longer necessary. Hastings parents pressed for proper secondary
education to be restored to the locality, so that their still evacuated
children could return. However, nobody was under the delusion that
the war was over and this was brought home by the testing, in early
August, of the additional air raid warning. The simple message to
residents was: ignore the 'cuckoo' alert and you court disaster.

Britain's agricultural productivity continued dramatically above pre-
war levels and the 1943 harvest was a good one. The war had
completely changed the British landscape; before the war there were
17 million acres of grazing land and 12 million of arable land but the
effects of WWII reversed the position. The German U-boat blockade,
which inhibited imports, made it imperative for Britain to produce
more of its own food. The chalky soil of the South Downs was put to
the plough, thus endangering flora and fauna, hedgerows were
removed to enlarge fields and more fertilizers were used to increase
crop yields. Hastings is surrounded by farmland and so the weekly
news often had an agricultural slant.

1943

Women have worked the land with men since time immemorial, but the inception of the Women's Land Army earned their position a new respect. They took on increasingly more jobs traditionally associated with men. The East Sussex War Agricultural Executive Committee opened a thatching school for members of the WLA, saying the skill provided a healthy and interesting job, vital to the war effort. The women were given a four to six weeks course by an old hand, Mr M Harmer, who said, a bit discouragingly, that a thatcher was born, not made. At the end of the course the successful trainees would be able to thatch a haystack from start to finish.

Dear Hannah,
The most important parts of my shopping list these days are the vegetables and what your father calls my 'hippie food'. During the war, home produce was a major component of my diet; our own humble back garden was turned over to growing vegetables, with just a few patches of flowers. Many people had allotments and, complete with their little sheds and the congenial company of other growers, these plots became a thriving source of food and a social life. My father turned large areas of his several employers' ornamental gardens into vegetable plots, which yielded far more than the resident household could use, so some of it came our way. It was an unchallenged principle in our home that the men of the family were entitled to the biggest share of the meat ration, because they worked. But sometimes, the men would take a lunch packet to work that consisted of sandwiches of sliced beetroot or cold, new potatoes. One source of protein for my mother and I was soup, made from bone or vegetable stock and dried peas and lentils. She made delicious salads, the ingredients for which were often picked from the garden, just before use. In my old age I have reverted to this way of eating and it suits me very well. I wonder if the peace-loving, adult hippies of the sixties came about as a result of their being fed on a low-meat diet as children? No doubt a university will get a huge grant to investigate this before long!
Much Love From Gran'ma

By early September Italy was out of the war. Germany's former ally surrendered its forces unconditionally. The news of Italy's surrender was greeted with quiet satisfaction in Hastings and the feeling that it

119

was a great stride on the road towards victory. The popular expression, 'Don't you know there's a war on?' was still asked, in response to moans about shortages and restrictions but now, slipping in to conversations was, 'When the war is over.' Hastings and St. Leonards Chess Club members suggested, at its October AGM, that when peace was declared they should be the first to arrange a Victory Chess Congress of allied nations.

On 19th October, the exchange of sick and seriously wounded British and German prisoners of war began at the Swedish port of Gothenburg. Many of the British had been taken prisoner at Dunkirk in 1940, others, including Canadians, had been captured at the Dieppe raid in 1942. Several Hastings families received news that their men had been chosen for the exchange; one was NCO Staff Sergeant John Huggins, of 54 Greville Road. To celebrate his return, bunting and flags were strung across the street and a 'Welcome Home' sign was fixed to the front door of his house, where his wife and sons, aged 27 and 18, and his daughter, 12, greeted him. Sergeant Huggins still had in his wallet a cloverleaf, sent to him in a letter by his daughter and carried throughout his captivity. He had been captured in Greece in 1941 and, including his military service, had been away from home for a total of four years. He was a regular soldier in WWI and before re-enlisting in 1940, he had served in the Civil Defence. He said of his time as a prisoner, "The Germans treated us with respect and the officers in charge helped us with arranging sports and entertainments. Their doctors and nurses cared for us well, in various hospitals". He added that the RAF was careful to avoid bombing hospitals and civilian areas and, 'German civil morale is low, they know they are beaten'. The Hastings and St Leonards British Legion gave a welcome home party to the returned POWs in Haig House.

The town marked the 24th Armistice Day with a church service, a march past, the laying of poppy wreathes at the Alexandra Park War Memorial and the observation of two minutes silence. Social events were held to raise money for the Poppy Day Fund. From the lower slopes of Mount Etna, Italy, a British soldier sent a consignment of lemons and almonds, which was one of the prizes in a Poppy Day raffle that raised £931. The nation was still pre-occupied with scrap collecting and people were asked to return their poppies, so that they could be refurbished for re-use or salvaged.

Hastings National Savings total for week December 11th 1943 was £8,147. In the light of Hastings' poverty and the wartime shortages, the Christmas warning by The National Savings Committee to, "Beware the Squander Bug, Hitler's secret weapon" seemed hardly necessary. There was very little on which to squander money, as the pre-Christmas advertising showed. The most mundane of items were suggested as gifts; a tea cosy, two fabric covered coat hangers, a feather duster or that good old Christmas standby, handkerchiefs. For the forces these were available in khaki or air force blue. The nearest thing to luxury was a box of four handkerchiefs of finest cotton, edged with lace, costing 6/3d (31½ p).

1943

Emile Crane wrote her Christmas letter from Lavender Cottage to thank her benefactors for their generosity:

Lavender Cottage.   December 18th 1943.

Dear Marion,

You can't imagine what a delightful surprise when the postman came and handed me your parcel. I forgot all about being tired in my eagerness to open it. It was a joy! I marvelled especially at the way you had remembered the little things that one cannot get here; you will know those to which I refer, even though I don't mention them, but I am sure the censor would not object. My two friends gazed longingly at the cake, not having seen such for many months, but I was quite firm and said, " Not until Christmas Day, and if we can wheedle the butcher into giving us some suet and save the fat from our weekly rations, we can have a real Christmas Pudding with the raisins." I had much bother in preventing them from eating the latter. I can understand it, as dried fruit is most hard to get, except from the black market. I liked too, the little Christmas adornments on the parcels.

We have asked two invalid friends for Christmas Day and shall be able to give them a very nice dinner, thanks to you. The butcher promises mutton, he suggested pork but that is not suitable for invalids. Poultry is out of the question; I heard turkeys are selling at £5 each and chickens at 30 shillings or two pounds. It is outrageous but they say they can't get the feed for the birds. Of course the troops get the best food, which is as it should be. We are fortunate in having the garden, as vegetables are such a good standby.

We have had quite a peaceful time here of late, with only occasional dives for the shelter and we hope this will last until Christmas is over at any rate. Things look hopeful don't they? But we try not to be over-optimistic, in accordance with Churchill's instructions. My very best thanks again for the lovely parcel and I write love and every good wish to you,
Yours affectionately, Emilie.
The week that Emilie posted her letter, Hastings Food Control Committee announced that the prospect of buying a turkey for

1943

Christmas in Hastings was discouraging. Butcher, Councillor Rymill said, 'People have been selling birds haphazardly, nobody knows where poultry is coming from, control should go through the proper channels. Unless something is done people are going to be without poultry and rabbits this Christmas'. Concern was also raised that cabbages, sold by allotment holders for one penny, had slipped past the attention of the Food Control Committee and were re-appearing in shops for as much as 7d or 8d (3½ p) each. In an attempt at Christmas jollity the Ministry of Food contributed to the family fun with a cut out and keep, wartime food quiz: 'Why do children need cod liver oil? What is the correct way to cook greens? What are the point's values of the following foods? What is the fresh equivalent of a packet of dried egg? What time is the broadcast of the BBC radio programme, The Kitchen Front?' The last, a real brain-teaser, 'How do you clean old cooking fat?'

Dear Hannah,

The stresses of war and the nightly air raids were taking their toll on my parent's marriage. One son was in constant danger at sea, while the other was still weak from a long illness. Ron had been discharged from the hospital in the spring. He was painfully thin, with arms that did not function properly and a whispery voice. To give my mother a rest, I was sent to Mrs West in Somerset and Ron was designated to be my chaperone on the train journey; he had to wear many layers of hard to come by clothes, to keep his frail body warm. The journey seemed endless to me and at one point I asked my brother if we could be getting near Germany yet, as this was the farthest point I was aware of those days. As soon as Ron left me, home sickness set in and I was a tiresome guest. I recall that with the help of the 12 year-old son of the house I managed to set fire to the artificial Christmas tree, while we were experimenting with candles. A cat scratch on my hand became extremely painful and swollen and an interesting red line ran up my arm from the source of infection, No penicillin for me, just a series bread poultices. When my mother got news of this she grew alarmed and I went back to Chislehurst. Regardless of air raids and my parent's continuing rows, it was wonderful to be home

With very Much Love Gran'ma.

1944

A prominent Hastings citizen was seriously injured in a bomb attack in the first week of 1944. Local surgeon, David Ligat, aged 72, arrived at his home in Filsham Road, after carrying out an emergency operation at a local hospital. He had just garaged his car, when a bomb fell in open ground near his house. The blast tore off his right arm and he was rushed back to the hospital he had just left. According to a newspaper report, Mr Ligat calmly gave directions for his own treatment, cheerfully making light of his injury by saying, 'Well, that's finished my golf". Hastings Town Clerk appealed to boys of 15 and girls of 16 to come forward to enrol in a messenger pool; in the event of a breakdown in telephone communications, emergency services would be paralysed and runners would be needed. At the end of January a Hastings fireman found a young German airman hiding in a vicarage front garden; he was one of the crew that had baled out of an aircraft that had been shot down over the sea. Another German from the same aircraft was captured just outside Hastings, near a sand quarry. Both men were wet and cold and without boots, neither put up any resistance. Their captors seem to have treated them kindly, providing blankets and the British panacea to all ills, a cup of tea.

During the course of the war the government never seemed to run out of schemes to raise money and highlight the civilian's awareness of the part they could play in achieving victory. Hastings' Mayor, as part of a nationwide drive, accepted a challenge to collect 75,000 unwanted books, magazines and periodicals in a fortnight. The books were to be scrutinised by a competent committee and then allocated as reading material to the forces, to restock blitzed libraries or to be pulped for munitions. School children were the official collectors of books, dropping them off at designated centres. The record for the greatest number of books deposited, 3,543, was held by retired grocer, Mr Feery, who turned his house into a receiving office. The total of books collected for Hastings was 100,000, all the more remarkable as this was during a period of snow and few people had transport.

Dear Hannah,

The news item about the book-collecting drive re-awakened memories of my being involved in this event whilst a pupil at the Annunciation School, in Chislehurst. There was an award system for the number of

books collected, based on military ranks. I had developed a passion for books but, due to lack of money and wartime shortages, there were never enough to satisfy my craving. As much as I enjoyed the children's favourites from the lending library, I longed for something meatier. I sometimes strayed into the adult's section of the library to browse but at Chislehurst Library it was strictly forbidden for children to borrow grownup's books. For me to have a perfectly valid reason to go and ask people to give me books was a chance not to be missed. Before passing them on to the school's collection I read as many as I could. I particularly remember Tarzan of the Apes and The Stars Look Down. I regret I never rose beyond a 'private' in the book collector ranks and I felt a bit guilty at my poor showing. Your mother and her family are very keen readers and your father could read by the time he was three. In the hope you will follow both families' footstep a baby's library was in the making even before you were born. We are all longing to read to you!
With Very Much Love, Gran'ma.

On 8th March, a dramatic fire, in no way connected with the war, brought hundreds of onlookers onto the seafront in the evening, to watch a spectacular blaze on St Leonards Pier. The local, National Fire Service, now well trained by the demands of air raids, extinguished the fire. The pier had already deteriorated considerably over the years due to weather and neglect. The first pile for its construction was driven in on March 1st 1888 and the pier was finally demolished in 1957, as it had become a hazardous structure.

On March 12th 1944, the town suffered a raid in the small hours of Sunday morning, during which a house, opposite to Emmanuel Church, was demolished by a direct hit. It was the home of the gifted Hastings artist and Municipal College teacher, Leslie Badham; his daughter was killed and his wife escaped serous injury but Mr Badham died shortly after being rescued.

For months, the nation's thoughts had been occupied with the invasion of Europe that was sure to come. From 1st April, Hastings was again a banned area; this extended 10 miles inland and all along the coast from The Wash to Land's End. The importance of carrying identity cards at all times was re-emphasised and only authorised persons could use binoculars and telescopes. Former BBC announcer Bruce Belfrage, RNVR, paid a visit to the town, to address the Civil Defence Services on how careless talk could affect the outcome of the invasion. He illustrated his theme with a film that showed how one overheard remark or a series of leaked and apparently unconnected fragments of information could be highly dangerous to national security, if they fell upon enemy ears. He said: "The German Intelligence is interested in the coming invasion; they want to know when, where, how and in what strength".

John Bryant was in the RAF in WWII and he trained as a Radar Operator. He said: "Our job was to detect and track down the position of aircraft in the Bristol Channel. All information was passed to an underground operations centre. There was a chain of stations all round Great Britain, with a central headquarters, where they would be aware of all aircraft, both friendly and hostile, all around the coast. Radar was a comparatively new invention; it was by no means perfect and its success was largely due to there being a number of stations with overlapping coverage, so that an average reading could be taken from several stations. We had one of the first automatic calculators, which would show us the position of aircraft on the map, after the direction and range were fed into them. The mechanics of this vast device occupied two rooms and as it operated, huge components clanged in all directions.

John Bryant

After months of training and exercises all over England, we arrived at Hastings and set up our equipment on a cliff-top golf course for a few weeks. It was beautiful weather and the town was almost deserted, as it was a banned area. At that time no unauthorised visitors were allowed within ten miles of the coast and the shops had goods unobtainable elsewhere. I recall they had good stocks of Brylcreem, which was in short supply elsewhere. My main memory is of the generous hospitality of the Hastings people. A friend and I attended Sunday Evensong at St Clement's Church and at the end of the service a Mr Fryatt asked if we would like to take 'pot luck' for supper at his home. We were invited there several times.

One rather frightening memory: A few of us were in a group, talking on the cliffs golf course, when there was a rushing sound and a thud. A bomb disposal group was sent for and they found a gigantic piece of shrapnel, embedded in the ground; it had missed me by inches. We discovered later that the shrapnel had become lodged in one of our bombers during an air raid over Germany but it had worked loose, when the plane was crossing our coast. Our bomb disposal people said that they would forward the shrapnel for examination, as it was possible to ascertain from it what materials the Germans were using, those that were in short supply and what substitutes they were deploying".

Salute the Soldier National Savings Week was launched on 13th May, with a target of £400,000, the cost of equipping and maintaining the Cinque Ports Battalion of the Royal Sussex Regiment for one year. The slogan was, 'Save and lend for those you know and love!' People were asked to 'Put out flags and banners to make the Salute the Soldier week bright and gay'. On Friday 12th May, Winston Churchill, accompanied by McKenzie King, PM of Canada and General Smuts, PM of South Africa made an unannounced (for security reasons) visit to Hastings. Churchill, as Lord Warden of the Cinque Ports and Colonel of the Royal Sussex Regiment, had particular connections with the region. Quite by chance Noel Care saw these notables when he was going home from work: "I was near the castle on the West Hill, when I noticed some parked limousines and a number of people standing around. A policeman told me that Churchill, some Colonial Prime Ministers and high ranking officers were visiting the town and that they were on the cliffs, watching training and visiting Hastings Castle and if I waited, I would see them. Soon, a group of gentlemen appeared from the direction of the castle; I recognised Churchill and Smuts, the faces of others were familiar but I could not name them. Churchill was smiling broadly and seemed in the best of spirits" What was not generally known at the time was that one of the ATS officers on the West Hill, Ack-Ack gun site was Churchill's daughter, Mary. Lord Kindersly launched the week's fund raising programme the next day;

his wife was presented with a bouquet by a shy three year old, William Winston White. Before the week was over the target sum was passed and a new aim was set, to try and better the £521,000 that had been raised for Wings for Victory Week. The final sum raised for Salute the Soldier Week was £542,000.

John Bryant's RAF unit moved on to Seaford Head, he said. "We assembled our equipment close to the cliff's edge and lived, cooked and slept in tents. Our job was to control fighter aircraft and direct them onto enemy targets. There were other troops there, including Americans. We remained there, waiting the call to join the European invasion force. During our time off we were able to visit Eastbourne and Brighton. I also have happy memories of the small seaside town of Seaford; there was a Women's Voluntary Service canteen, which was used by both British and American Servicemen. In the evenings the streets were full of servicemen enjoying the peace of a pleasant spring but the tranquillity was not to last. The atmosphere soon became electric, as everyone was waiting the word to go. In the days leading up to D Day we could see barges loading with troops at Newhaven and early on 6th June, there was a constant stream of aircraft heading towards France. Early morning news bulletins told of landings and there were inspiring messages from war leaders. Our padre held an impromptu service in the YMCA canteen, to pray for the troops, who were at that moment fighting in Normandy. We later went into Brighton, where excitement was at fever pitch. Our sister unit was called to operate on the Normandy beaches; it was there for several hours, bombarded by heavy guns and it suffered serious casualties".

Fifty years on, in June 1994, the country commemorated D-Day and the Hastings Observer sought out local veterans, to recount their experiences of the landing and battle. Former Sherman Tank Driver Jack Jarman who was 24 when he took part in the invasion, said he still had the leaflet that the troops were given just before crossing the channel, to land on the perilous beaches. The leaflet was a pre-battle call for victory from General Eisenhower but Jack, who had already faced the horrors of Dunkirk and had fought in the Middle East, said the words did little to improve his morale. Laddie Hitchman was 20 when he became one of the thousands who landed on the beaches in a hail of fire. He said that the memories of it have overshadowed the rest of his life and he is haunted by the things he did and saw on Sword Beach. Of the ceremonies to mark the half-centenary of the battle he said; "I am not interested in shows or events, every year I go back across the water to see my mates' graves". His old army pal Frank Baldwin said: "We knew something big was coming up two days before D-Day. On the ship there was a sense of anticipation but nobody really knew what to expect. We came in view of the beaches at 7.30am and we had to wade the last 50 yards. There wasn't time to look around us and I don't remember the huge Armada they said was there. We braved machine guns and shells to get to the shelter of the sand dunes; it was an exciting but terrible experience. Men were falling everywhere. When I stopped to help a very seriously injured man I was told to move on. Later I saw my best mate killed." Fred Petrie, of the 553 Field Company of the Royal Engineers, remembered seeing the Mulberry Harbours being towed across the southern horizon off Hastings. He spent his last night in his hometown before going to join his regiment. He recalled the supper he had; "It was corned beef pie and mash and in spite of the stress I was in high spirits. I went out with my girlfriend, who was in the ATS and billeted at Sandrock Hall and we put a top hat on the statue of Queen Victoria that stands in Warrior Square". Ray Gladwish, a former Hastings and St Leonards Sea Cadet, was also part of the preliminaries to the D-Day invasion, when his ship, HMS Speedwell, swept the landing coast from Le Havre to Cherbourg.

Bob Champion has a vivid memory of the day before D-Day: "The fields opposite to where I lived, in Lower Lake, Battle, were packed with bell tents, literally hundreds of them, all occupied by soldiers of the Somerset Light Infantry. When my friends and I went over there on the morning of 6th June the whole area was completely deserted, all the soldiers had gone to take part in the landing. It was quite uncanny, as on the previous night it had been teeming with people. They had left behind all sorts of personal things, shoes, clothing and even money.

Dear Hannah,

Isn't the name Mulberry Harbour attractive? You would never imagine their grim purpose. They were floating harbours that were built to assist with the D-day landings in France. During the Normandy Invasion it was necessary for vast supplies of men, equipment and stores to be brought ashore quickly on the French coast. The real harbours were heavily defended and the beaches unfit for landings. Each Mulberry Harbour was constructed mainly of floating, reinforced concrete blocks. On D-Day these were linked to form 2 separate harbours. To anchor the harbours and to protect them from being broken up in rough seas, almost 60 merchant ships had been sunk. I understand that some of the components that made up the harbour could not be moved for various reasons and are still lying off the Normandy coast, serving as an historical monument to D-Day.

I was amused to read about a departing soldier putting the top hat on Queen Victoria. She is still similarly disrespected these days; only it's usually a traffic cone at New Year's Eve. She suffered the greatest indignity when she was shot through the skirt by a German machine gun bullet in WWII. The statue and plinth underwent a major clean up about two years ago and I was so pleased there was no attempt to repair the bullet hole, which has become a part of local history.

Some years ago I came to know a Hastings antique and collectibles dealer, born into the Hastings fishing community on 6th June 1944. He was given a name that would cause comment for his entire life. He told me: "My father Albert George White had three sons, Bertie, Kenny and myself. Bertie and my father were fishermen and crewed on the Hastings Lifeboat. In the war my father was in a reserved occupation, as he was both fisherman and lifeboat man. When I was expected, my father put up a list in The Royal Standard pub to invite suggestions for a name for the new baby. I was born on 6th June 1944, so the top suggestion was D-Day, the code name for the invasion of occupied Europe. This was much to my Mum's surprise. Two days later, my Dad went to register the birth of his son with the name of D-Day. The registrar said that name could not be used, as it was a military secret. So my father showed him the newspaper headlines, 'Second Day of D-Day', and asked him how much of a secret is that? However, he compromised by putting double e in DeeDay and the registrar accepted it. HMS Rowney was one of the first boats to open up the D-Day bombardment, hence my middle name of Rowney". DeeDay has passed on this unique name to his own son, who eventually joined the

army. His dad said he would understand if he wanted to change his name but it proved to be no problem. DeeDay Junior said: "Everyone else has been given nicknames but I was born with mine"!
When you are old enough, Hannah, I will take you to see DeeDay's fascinating shop in the Old Town.

With very Much Love, Gran'ma

It had been feared that the invasion would bring forth an enemy blitz on the coastal towns but this did not happen. Instead Hitler had a nasty surprise for the British, as Joyce Brewer remembers: "We began to think our troubles might be over after the invasion of Europe and hopefully, the end of the war was in sight. But then there came another menace, the V1 or, as we called them, the doodlebugs. They looked like a small plane with short wings, a jet engine at the rear, a huge explosive charge in the nose and NO pilot. They were launched from ramp sites in France and Belgium and it did not take them long to wing their way across the English Channel and head for their intended target -London. The first we knew of them was on 14th June, when the first one came over; the AA gun sites were given the code name for them, 'Diver-Diver'. The following night my two future brothers-in-law, Jim and Jack, were having supper with us, when the sirens sounded and then we heard this awful chugging sound in the sky above us. We ran to the front door, the weather was overcast with drizzly rain and we saw the first doodlebug flew in low, over the houses in Mount Pleasant Road. Not that we could see the doodlebug's shape in the dark, just a jet of flame and this horrible, unforgettable racket. Jim rushed to the Bofors gun and Jack dived into the bucket seat of the twin Browning machine guns, situated just across the road from our house. He was not a happy man when he sat in a puddle of water, as he was wearing his best uniform. He opened fire immediately and hit an electricity pylon in Fir Tree Road and scared the daylights out of a passer-by; the robot machine went on unscathed. After all of our previous experiences this came as another shock to our nervous systems, I felt sick with fright and buried my head in the pillow, but it did not block out the noise and needless to say, we slept very badly that night, as more 'bugs' came over. And that was how things continued for the next two months. Thousands of them were launched and hundreds flew over Hastings; on occasions as many as six could be seen at one time. This part of southern England became known as 'Doodlebug Alley'. All kinds of defences were installed to combat them. These included heavy and light batteries of guns, barrage balloons and the fighter planes that were fast enough to catch them; Spitfires, Tempests Typhoons, P38 Lightning's and P47 Thunderbolts. On the East and West Hill and all along the seafront, guns pointed out to sea. The cost in ammunitions must have been terrible, considering the barrage that was put up. At night it looked like a huge firework display, with shells exploding all around those fiery monsters. Red-hot, jagged lumps of shrapnel dropped to the ground, the only safe place to be was in the air-raid shelter; believe me, it wasn't fun.

As the gunners became more experienced, their success rate improved but inevitably, not all the doodlebugs were shot down into the sea, some landed on the town, causing death and injury and severe damage to property. The RAF planes were very effective too, they downed hundreds with cannon fire and some very brave pilots flew alongside the bugs and, with their planes' wing, tipped them off-balance, to upset their gyroscope, which sent them diving to the earth. The RAF pilots had orders to bring the Doodlebugs down on open land if possible and they downed 374 in the rural area outside Hastings but some fell on isolated farms and cottages, causing casualties. While all this was going on, I had to continue with my war work, delivering the rations of milk to the Hastings people, as bullets and shrapnel were clattering down on my milk van's flimsy, tarpaulin roof. I felt very vulnerable and often borrowed my Dad's tin hat when he wasn't at work. I vividly remember one particular day: I decided to alter my round and was in Fairlight Road when a doodlebug was hit by shellfire, directly overhead and it dived towards Ore Valley, near my home, and exploded with a huge bang. Worried to death for my Mum and family, I drove straight home to find them safe and sound but worried about me. The bomb had landed in nearby Pine Avenue, causing casualties and damage to the house next to where I should have been, if I hadn't changed my route.

Joyce Brewer

Another time, we were seated

at the table, enjoying something special that Mum had concocted from our meagre rations; she declared we wouldn't let anything spoil our meal. Some hope! We heard the buzz, then planes and machine-gun fire, so we rushed to the door just in time to see a P38 Lightning explode a doodlebug over the town. There was a huge bang and a big black cloud and shock waves that made the windows rattle; one less to fall on London.

One night, 'our gun' scored a hit and the 'bug turned a somersault and headed back out to sea. I actually saw a doodlebug released from a plane inland; the Germans were experimenting with carrying them slung under the fuselage of Junkers 88 bombers but thank goodness it didn't prove to be very successful. It was scary enough when they came from the seaward direction. During this period we used to sleep downstairs on mattresses; this would not have saved us during a direct hit but it gave us a small sense of security. Not for me though, I could tell when a doodlebug was heading our way long before it arrived because the sound waves were transmitted through the seabed, as they flew over the Channel. I guess it was similar to how the American Native Indians used to put their ears to the ground, to listen for approaching horses.

It wasn't a happy time but we made our amusements at home, listening to the radio, playing family games and having hobbies; mine were painting and drawing. We rarely went to the cinema; they were not good places to be when the raids were on. The Plaza had received a direct hit and other cinemas had near misses. My sister Barbara and her boyfriend Jack took my mother to the Ritz Cinema one afternoon to see 'Gone with the Wind'. During the film, an actor said, 'Hark, the guns!' just as heavy guns on Hastings' West Hill opened fire. Mum looked at Jack but he looked fixedly at the screen and didn't move, so she took her cue from him. Of course he was scared but being a soldier he had to set a good example- good old Jack!"

Dear Hannah.

Everyone old enough to remember has a story about the night the doodlebug attacks started. For me it began with the familiar and miserable routine of being roused from sleep by my anxious mother, at the start of an air raid. We had no air raid shelter of our own so shared our neighbour's, which was one of the surface standing, brick variety. It lacked any comforts and I was told to sit on an upturned bucket. What we thought were aeroplanes kept passing overhead with alarming frequency. They sounded completely different from any we had heard before, a rattling, old motorbike roar, which would suddenly cut out, to be followed moments later by an explosion. My father went outside the shelter repeatedly, to try and fathom what the pilots of this new aircraft were doing, why there was fire streaming from the tail and why the engines were stopping. I felt frightened and cold but my strongest memory is of the agony of the sharp, metal rim of the bucket, cutting into my scrawny backside. This night was the start of a most terrifying part of the war. We lived on the outskirts of London, directly under the doodlebug flight paths and the constant attacks from this monstrous weapon dominated our nights and days.

The family that was employing my parents as cook/cleaner and gardener found it too much to bear and they fled to the countryside. They were fearful that their property would be looted, so they asked my parents to live in, as caretakers. Overnight, our humble life-style changed to one of upper middle class comfort. The employer was a stockbroker, so our new home was a large detached residence in leafy, secluded Holbrooke Lane, in Chislehurst. The house had every convenience and many rooms; a billiard and music room, with a highly polished floor for dance parties, a sumptuous drawing room, furnished with soft, chintz-covered settees and armchairs and an imposing dining room, full of well cared for antiques. The youngest child in the family, a boy, a few years older than me, had an airy, sunny bedroom and a separate bathroom and playroom, with lots of toys and, best of all, a library! There was a big garage, and here too was an assortment of playthings, including bicycles, a scooter, and equipment for croquet and tennis. At the end of the garden stood a privet-hedge maze and beyond it was a large sandpit and Wendy House. My mother's domain was a spacious kitchen, with separate scullery and pantry, where stood the pre-war emblem of wealth, a refrigerator! A two-tier Morrison Shelter was installed for us in the kitchen, where we were supposed to live our daily lives. Do you think we did? More of that later!

With Very Much Love, Gran'ma

Monica found another farm job at Westfield, a four and a half mile bike ride away from her home: "The village shop allowed me to borrow their old sit-up-and-beg-bike for this journey. During the ride there was an excitingly steep valley and I would shoot down it at such a rate that the impetus would take me half way up the other side. The work on this farm was different, the cows were milked by hand but I worked with another girl, two years my senior. We got on well and had lots of fun, along with plenty of hard work. It was on my way to work in mid-June 1944 that I saw my first V1 or doodlebug. It was my 16th birthday and as I cycled to work the air was heavy with the intoxicating scent of summer flowers and new mown hay. Then I saw what I thought was a damaged plane, with fire coming out of the back. I thought about the poor pilot and I hoped he would get home OK. Later that day I was to learn how wrong I had been and what it really was that I had seen. As weeks passed, we became very familiar with the wretched things. Every effort was made to prevent them from reaching their target and to shoot them down over open country. I saw this tactic in progress all too clearly. When I was working in the fields I saw three fighter planes, with guns blazing, trying to get a doodlebug down. It looked so close and I was terrified.

Eventually, the gunners succeeded, the missile's engine stopped and it fell two or three fields away but it sounded as if it was immediately overhead. The explosion made a crater in the soft soil deep enough for a double-decker bus. The doodlebugs persisted and it was not until our armies arrived at the launching sites that they ceased. Then poor old London had another horror, the V2s, which the RAF was unable to intercept. The village where I lived had a narrow escape in the early hours that summer, when one of these flying bombs came down on its outskirts. The blast damaged 40 houses, including ours; all of our doors and windows

Monica, on the farm.

were blown in, there was glass everywhere, tiles were stripped from our roof and exterior walls. As we sat having a cup of tea, the village vicar put his head through the gap where the window should have been and said, 'That's the spirit, we must keep going'! No person was killed in the explosion but a nearby farmer had the distressing experience of losing most of his cows; the herd had assembled by a gate, as they habitually did, waiting for milking time. They caught the full blast of the bomb, many were massacred and it took their owner a long time to recover from the shock".

Guns on St Leonards Seafront. Source: Hastings Museum.

Batteries of heavy AA guns were installed on the seafront at West Marina and on the Oval, above White Rock, to bring down the flying bombs, before they could reach London. Residents feared these defences were putting them in the front line and that the sound of the guns firing would be intolerable. There was also concern that the town would suffer a rain of shot-down doodlebugs. To reassure the townspeople and as an expression of goodwill, Hastings Mayor, in civic state, with full regalia and accompanied by an entourage of dignitaries, visited the gun sites. To quote the Hastings Observer: 'The civic attire and the 250 year old mace were in stark contrast to the grim line of heavy guns along the hillside, overlooking a peacetime golf course'. It was unfortunate that at

On Watch. Hastings East Hill. Pier and castle in background.
Source: Hastings Museum.

this time the Hastings Mayor was misquoted in a national press article, which gave the impression that he doubted the courage and endurance of the population of the town. A local, public outcry at this affront followed and gave some small distraction from the war.

Ivor White had taken a job as a cinema projectionist at the Senlac cinema in Battle and he gave this account of a very close sighting of a doodle bug: "I remember that it was still daylight on a summer evening in 1944, and I was taking a break from the cinema operating room. Between reels, it was our chosen duty to go out onto the flat roof above the Foyer and watch for signs of enemy activity in the skies overhead. We did not always get a warning siren during air raids and it was our practice to show a slide on the cinema screen, informing our audience of any possible danger, so that they could choose to stay in the building or seek shelter elsewhere. On this particular evening, I was out on the roof looking southwards, towards Hastings, when I heard the unmistakeable sound of a doodlebug. Almost immediately, I spotted the pilot-less aircraft coming straight towards me, at a height of approximately 2,000 feet, flames belching from the rear of the engine. My instant reaction was to duck, but then I realised that it was far too high to hit the cinema. I turned, keeping the doodlebug in my sight, and watched it disappear, out of view, heading north. Several seconds later, the engine stopped and I waited for the bang.

The following morning, I was informed that this V1 had hit the roof of my Aunt Annie's house in Dallington, just a few miles away from Battle, as a doodlebug flies. My Aunt Annie and my Uncle Dave had heard it coming and were quick enough to dive under their Morrison shelter, which undoubtedly saved their lives. The house was a wreck, and Annie and Dave were evacuated to a neighbour's house where they stayed until the end of the war. Their house, Highlands Villa, was eventually rebuilt to

Doddlebug over Battle Church. Image by Ivor White.

the original plans under a government, 'War Damage' scheme'.

Bob Champion was about 16 at the time of the doodlebugs and employed by a firm of joinery manufacturers. He said: "With three other men, I was working at the old bus depot in Bulverhythe, St. Leonards, which had been requisitioned by the Royal Army Ordnance Corps, for use as a workshop. The building was quite large, with a roof of two gables and the ridges on each gable had 8-foot glass inserts on both sides. It was our job to black out these windows with movable shutters, so that the army mechanics could work at night. On the day in question I had come down from the scaffolding, to go to the toilet, which was outside the main building. I had just reached the entrance when I heard a loud buzzing, and looking up I saw this doodlebug coming in low and as it seemed, straight toward me; I was transfixed, and unable to move. Then, to my horror, it flew between the bus depot's two gables. (It wasn't until much later that I realised that if it had been a few yards to the left or right, it would

Bob Champion on
National Service

have hit the building, and exploded immediately above me, and I wouldn't be here to tell the tale). After a few seconds elapsed, it exploded about 100 yards away, at Harley Shute. I believe it demolished a couple of houses. The depot's glass roof was shattered and it rained down on the soldiers working below, causing a number of casualties. Some were struck by the heavy, lead glazing bars but luckily there weren't any fatalities. The incident made such an impression on me that I can still picture it clearly to this day."

John Gill had been a Sea Cadet in 1939; their HQ was at the bathing Pool at West Marina, St Leonards. The cadets numbered about 300 at the time; many later went into the Royal Navy, through what was known as the Bounty Scheme. The bathing pool was ideal for their HQ. They did boat-work in the pool, the parade training on the top and middle decks and the classrooms were on the lower deck. The diving tower was used for lead -line training and signaling.

1944

John said, "I was evacuated for two separate periods, from summer 1940, finally returning late in 1943. I then went to Tower Road emergency school, where I remained until April 1944, when I left school and joined the GPO, as a boy messenger. In those days there were anti aircraft guns on the western seafront at Marina. One of our pastimes was collecting shrapnel from the spent ack-ack shells, which could be found all along the seafront, in the road and on the pavement.

It was about this time that I recall seeing the first flying bomb from my bedroom window, which faced north. We thought at the time that it was an

John Gill on duty as GPO Messenger

aircraft on fire because there were flames coming from the rear. It wasn't until we read in the newspaper the following morning that we learned it was a rocket-propelled, un-manned aircraft/bomb. There was a full description and diagrams showing how the machine worked. The sound the V1 made was un-mistakable. If the sound suddenly cut out then one ran for cover because it was about to fall to earth and explode. The ack-ack guns used to try and shoot them down.

When I worked as a messenger, we went each day to a community kitchen at Tower Road School for our lunch. We were given vouchers and did not have to pay. One of the more unpleasant tasks we messenger boys had to do was to deliver telegrams, which notified of the death of sons or husbands serving in the forces. Occasionally, we conveyed happier news. I recall delivering a telegram to a lady, whose husband had been reported missing in action a couple of years previously. The telegram informed her that her husband was a prisoner of war in Japanese hands. It so happened that this lady's husband was a Post Office employee before the war and he eventually came back to work for a while, as my overseer".

One Sunday afternoon 16th July, fighters hit a flying bomb they were chasing and it fell among houses in Hollington Old Lane and Church Road. Two houses were demolished and many others heavily damaged, with debris thrown over a wide area. Three people were killed in the incident and 47 were injured, 12 seriously. Francis Cornwall, an Evening Argus reporter since 1930, served abroad with the Royal Corp of Signals during the entire war. He contributed a detail from his late wife's experience of this raid: "My wife, Louie, was renting a house in Battle Road, St Leonards and during the 16th July raid, she and her mother took cover in their Morrison Shelter, when a flying bomb crashed and demolished houses and damaged many up to 200 yards away. The blast blew out the sitting room window frame and also the pantry window, ruining their food". During an earlier air raid, Frances Cornwall's Aunt Florence had been instantly killed in September 1940, on her front step in St Peter's Road. She had been on her way out but retraced her steps, to alert the elderly lady occupant of the top flat, who survived the raid. Francis said that he thought that the men who were overseas did not always appreciate what their womenfolk were going through at home.

John Bryant's unit remained on Seaford Head for several weeks, awaiting the call to Normandy. He said of that time: "Our comparative peace was shattered by the first flying bomb. We did not know what it was, it sounded like a broken-down motorbike. It was soon identified and many more arrived in a steady stream, sometimes all night. The doodlebugs would come in over the sea very low, perhaps at 100 feet. The anti-aircraft gun would open up and, as it tracked the V1's course over land, we were exposed to our own gunfire. We had no protection and so we hurriedly dug trenches and installed a siren. On one occasion I saw a V1 coming in very close so I dived under a lorry for protection and as I looked out I could see an RAF fighter, lights winking along its wings, chasing the rocket. There were machine gun bullets flying everywhere; next day my friend found an unexploded cannon shell in his kitbag. The V1s were very fast; so modified Spitfires and Tempest aircraft deployed the tactic of waiting at a high altitude and then diving to generate sufficient speed to enable them to intercept the rockets. The Tempest aircraft, coupled with their pilots' skills, proved to be very adept at downing doodlebugs and they accounted for one third of those shot down". Eventually, the call came for John Bryant's unit to go to Portsmouth, where they were loaded onto landing craft tanks for a rough crossing to Normandy. The night after they arrived there was a very heavy RAF raid on Le Havre and as they moved northwards the Allies 1,000-bomber raids were frequently occurring. Their radar tubes were filled with evidence of these and it was sometimes difficult to pick out the fighters they were controlling. John said: "We served in France, Belgium and Holland and went into Germany, a few days before the war ended. We saw plenty of action and devastation but I think that for me, the events at Seaford were more than comparable with these. During the V1 attacks we thought that our last moments had come and we were really very fortunate to survive".

Dear Hannah,

I recall the summer of 1944 as being a relatively happy one for me, in spite of the doodlebugs. My most enjoyable hours were spent in the library of our new home. I found on its shelves a complete set of Richmael Crompton's William Brown books and laughed out loud for the first time when reading. There were copies of the classic fairy tales, with beautiful illustrations. I opened George MacDonald's The Princess and the Goblin and The Princess and Curdie and discovered the rapt experience of reading books you can't put down. I heard recently, on BBC Radio 4 that some people keep a dairy of every book they have read. I wonder, Hannah, if you would want to do that. I will give a book to your mother at Christmas and she may like to start you off. How I wish I had kept one!

My pleasures were not solely reading. I would push the absent boy's scooter to the very end of the gently sloping Holbrook Lane and blissfully glide back down, keeping balance all the way. The refined residents complained to my parents about this ruffian's behaviour. I continued gliding, undeterred and concluded that the scooter's owner must be a sissy if he had not done it too. I banged about on the lawns with my own versions of tennis and croquet and indoors, I banged with similar enthusiasm on the piano in the music room, singing loudly, occasionally taking breaks for sliding sessions on the highly polished dance floor. My father kept the gardens in a state of order and beauty and here I cheerfully rode a bike round the pebbled paths, making him angry when I splattered small stones on the neat lawns. I would then retreat to the house, choosing any of the gracious rooms that took my fancy, to sprawl on the comfortable furniture and read and read.

1944

The war had certainly not gone away and the doodlebug attacks went on. One afternoon, as I was playing in the sandpit at the end of the garden a soft swishing sound made me look up, to see a doodlebug, its engine cut off, coasting just above the garden's tall trees. It continued its course and exploded some distance away. We suffered an even closer call during my Aunt Kit's weekly visit, when a doodlebug exploded in the garden of a house in Holbrook Lane. It was customary in those days for ladies to wear their hats throughout an afternoon tea visit and the kitchen ceiling fell on Aunt Kit's flower decorated, summer straw. She was so angry at it being ruined she screamed unladylike profanities at Hitler and all his generals!

Before the summer was over, my brother Derrick came on leave from the navy and he got engaged. Our borrowed home offered a perfect venue for a party and there certainly was one! I do not know how my mother found the ingredients but she made a wonderful party feast, including a chocolate engagement cake, decorated with triangles of Mars Bars and sugared, jelly sweets. My wartime stomach was unused to such excesses and I had my first bilious attack that night, followed almost immediately by mumps. It was at that point the stockbroker and his family decided to return home. As soon as the employer saw my swollen face I was exiled to an attic bedroom and complete isolation, to protect his young son and two grownup daughters. Thank goodness for the company of books and my wonderful 17 year-old brother, Ron. He had found a girl's dressing up box in the attic and on several evenings kept me laughing non-stop, as he appeared at my bedroom door, variously attired as a fairy, pixie, ballerina and a castanet-clacking, Spanish senorita. Hannah, your father has inherited this sense of fun and it pleases me no end to see him clowning about for your amusement, just as my brother did for me, so long ago.

The stockbroker finally allowed me to pass down the stairs but only if my face was completely covered by an antiseptic-soaked cloth. My recovery was the signal for us to go back to our own home and to a working class existence. Some of the things that had taken my childish fancy in that grand house were the decorative plates, hung on the walls by wire frames. I decided I would have those in my own house one day and now I have...Lots!

With Very Much Love, Gran'ma.

1944

Hastings and St Leonards neared the end of four years of air attacks when, on 29th July 1944, a flying bomb exploded on the steps of St Leonards Church, demolishing it and the neighbouring houses; this proved to be the last major incident caused by enemy bombing. On 25th August, to coincide with the lifting of the curfew, the ban on health and pleasure visits to Hastings was removed. These measures were expected to help the town start the recovery of its pre-war popularity and prosperity. Certain beaches remained closed, due to the danger of mines, and the War Office announced that the relaxing of these wartime regulations did not mean that there was less danger than previously from enemy missiles. Never the less, the public were quick to take advantage of the easing of restrictions and hundreds of day-trippers arrived by train and coach. The beaches were opened between Hastings Pier and Warrior Square and paddling, sand castle building and swimming were soon under way, for the first time in four years. For those few who wished to stay overnight there was sufficient accommodation.

In early September Hastings Corporation opened an information centre in the White Rock Pavilion and they were soon answering enquiries from holidaymakers and people who wished to open boarding houses in Hastings and St Leonards, after the war. The future for visitor accommodation in the town was giving concern. Many hotels and guesthouses had been requisitioned by the military and the government had been paying rent to the owners of the buildings. With the departure of the forces the property owners could de-requisition their establishments, which would then mean the loss of rent. Many properties had been left much in need of refurbishment and repair, servicemen in billets are not known for their careful ways! Much accommodation was not in a fit state for civilian guests and therefore, could not provide an income. To solve this problem the government offered hotel and guesthouse owners the equivalent of one year's rent.

By mid-September 1944 domestic blackout regulations were eased; the complete obscuration of lights was not required, only that the light be diffused by curtains. Street lighting was not resumed and so a rogue light, switched on by a fault, was a source of attraction in Bohemia. From the Hastings and St Leonards Observer: 'Passers-by stood enraptured, a mother brought her children from bed, to look at a wonderful sight they had never seen before, men left their beer and bus passengers gazed out as they drove through the pool of light and asked each other if the war was over. Then, two men from the electricity department, dressed in Home Guard uniform, arrived on a motor cycle and switched off the light that could not wait for victory'. By the end of that month restricted street lighting was approved and 12 streetlights were switched on in parts of the town centre.

Dear Hannah

It was not until after the doodlebug raids began that my family was given its two-tier Morrison Shelter. It was set in the fireplace corner and looked like a giant rabbit hutch, dominating our tiny sitting room. It was too high to serve as a table, in the way the single-decker model did and its top soon became an extension to our over-crowded mantelpiece. First the wireless was put on it, followed by an alarm clock, books, magazines, newspapers, a torch, candles and any other items needed in an emergency. Anything that fell down into the fireplace alcove behind the shelter was there for the duration of the war, unless it could be wangled out through the sturdy, metal mesh sides.

I found it rather cosy sleeping in the Morrison Shelter. Maybe it appealed to the primitive streak but the fact of us being together and safe in our 'cave' was very comforting. The room where it was installed was our only area for eating, hobbies and entertaining visitors. These were mostly male, my brothers' friends, or relatives. Card games, including cribbage, were a popular way of passing the time in our house and a group of young men, along with my father, would sit round the table, swapping jokes and smoking as they played cards and talked about their service life, work, the war or re-told the plot of a film they had just seen. This convivial, male company made me feel very safe, as I snuggled down in the Morrison Shelter, among clouds of cigarette smoke, lulled to sleep by gusts of male laughter. I have never smoked but still have no objection to the smell of cigarettes; it reminds me of those moments of security in a turbulent childhood.

Just when we thought the doodlebugs were over, Hitler launched his final weapon, the V2 rocket, which started falling in and around

1944

London in September 1944. The V2 was more accurate than the V1 and it lacked the frightening roar. It travelled 60 or 70 miles above the earth and at a speed faster than sound, so by the time it was audible it had crashed. Somehow, its silence seemed to make it less frightening than the V1, and people adopted the philosophical attitude that if you heard it coming you were ok and if you didn't, you were probably dead. Towards the end of 1944, my parents applied for a live in job, with a tied cottage, in the better part of Chislehurst, so it looked as if we might be on the move yet again.

With Very much Love, Gran'ma

Hastings announced the opening of the town's entire beach, from Rock-a-Nore to the Marina Bathing Pool on 14th October, the anniversary of the Battle of Hastings. As our troops advanced in Europe, the discovery of a vast store of German maps and plans indicated that the flat beaches of Hastings, Brighton and Littlehampton were to be used by enemy landing craft. The local authorities then revealed the previously secret plans for the compulsory evacuation of the entire civilian population of Hastings. Had the Germans invaded; only 1,000 Home Guard and Civil Defence members would remain. To speed the mass evacuation of civilians from Hastings, a timetable had been drawn up for departure by trains, each to carry 800 passengers away from the scene of impending invasion. Every aspect of the enforced departure was planned; records were kept of invalids and the chronically sick, who would need special arrangements, the Ministry of Food had made available a supply of emergency food for the evacuees, to cover a 48 hour period, and all domestic pets were to be destroyed. This plan was constantly revised throughout the war.

Hastings' evacuated families began to return to the town, some to find that their homes had been robbed of everything they contained; the risk of harsh penalties had not deterred looters from taking the almost irreplaceable furniture and chattels. Returnees whose houses had been demolished by bombing faced the problems of a shortage of housing and high rents.

The Home Guard was stood down and on 3rd December the members of the 23rd Sussex Battalion paraded through the town in front of

1944

crowds of hundreds of spectators, who had turned out in rough and wet weather, to witness this historic event. The oldest Home Guard who took part in the parade was Ex-Sergeant Major Crouch aged 74. 'Vigilant' wrote: 'They bore themselves with soldierly steadiness and made a worthy and dignified exit'. Nearly sixty years later, in November 2002, the Home Guard participated, for the very first time, in the Cenotaph Remembrance March Past. To Ivor White, former boy Home Guard went the honour of carrying the wreath of poppies, which he presented at the cenotaph steps. He said of this honour, with typical understatement, "I felt chuffed!" Ivor was not at home in 1944 to share a family Christmas, he said: "It was towards the end of the year that the important, brown envelope dropped onto the doormat of our house at 13, Senlac Gardens in Battle. After all my attempts to join the army as some kind of technician before my 18th birthday, I was quite disappointed to learn that the Irish Guards wanted me for a square-basher. Then I realised that the Guards had become mechanised, and maybe I was going to join my brother in the Guards Armoured Division. So, four days before Christmas, I turned up at The Guard's Depot, Caterham, in my Home Guard uniform, ready to 'do my duty' and pocket the Kings Shilling".

Some idea of the big change about to take place in Ivor's life on joining the Guards can be found in Keith Bryant's book, 'Fighting With the Guards', particularly the chapter, 'The Making of a Guardsman'. 'The new recruit, fresh from civilian life, has come from a background where the immaculate appearance of the space round his bed is not paramount. Nor does he associate old razor blades with floor scraping. So, before long he begins to feel he is in a crazy world, controlled by lunatics but every aspect of his training is designed to instill the essential qualities of discipline, physical fitness, self-esteem and pride in his regiment. Part of the discipline is order and cleanliness; the Guardsman's kit must be arranged in

Ivor White in the Irish Guards.

precise order at the head of his bed, the barrack room must shine like polished silver, the fire buckets like mirrors. Even the glass of the window by his bed must be polished daily, as are the ablutions and, to remove the slightest trace of dirt, the floors are scraped with razor blades. The Guardsman acquires fitness by a gruelling process of physical training and spending a great amount of time on the barrack square, learning precision drill, which is required so that he can fulfil royal household and ceremonial duties, for which the Guards are justly famous. The drill also plants quick and blind obedience in the Guardsman's mind.

After having met the high standards required, it is inevitable that the Guardsman begins to feel self-esteem. The reminders of his regiment's past glory, crests, names of battles and campaigns and the names of those who have won the Victoria Cross, surround him in his living quarters. All these he has to learn by heart and pride grows in him that he is part of this. The essential qualities will stand him in good stead in conflict; he will have been trained to regard no trouble too great, no matter how tired he may be. The Guardsman's drill develops unquestioning obedience that will make him hold firm in the disastrous stages of battle, yet swift to gain initiative. Efficiency and cleanliness are vital when handling weapons; a clean rifle will save his life and that of others, pride in his regiment and himself will reinforce his courage under fire; he has become part of a force of elite, fighting men'.

Dear Hannah.

When I read this piece about the making of a Guardsman I thought of my father, doing his Home Guard training with the Scots Guards, no wonder he suffered a rupture! My parents got the new job; it was with a family who lived in a house called Wood End, at the top of Logs Hill, between Chislehurst and Bromley. Our home was to be in the gardener's cottage, which, to my child's eye looked very like the Hansel and Gretel house, with its pretty, fretted gables and leaded windows. My parents were appointed as cook/housekeeper and gardener/handyman and we moved into the little cottage before Christmas. The gardens that surrounded the main house and cottage were beautiful; a large lawn for tennis, a rose garden, rangy rock gardens, dense shrubberies and a bluebell and chestnut tree spinney. Beside the kitchen garden stood a long greenhouse, where my father was to grow bedding and indoor plants, tomatoes, cucumbers, grapes, melons and peaches, fruits that I had never tasted. Our house move put me some considerable distance from my school. We juniors had made a premature move to Edgebury Secondary Modern, as the Annunciation School had been bombed. I did not mind the journey. A long walk to the bus stop took me past rich people's houses and gardens, a source of considerable interest to a gardener's daughter. The walk was followed by a bus ride through pretty Chislehurst Common.

We heard that shortly after we had left 27, Walden Avenue, a V2 rocket had hit one of the partially completed houses nearby and our former home had all its windows blown out and the ceilings fell down. Yet another of those 'what if' stories that became a part of people's wartime history.

With very Much Love, Gran'ma.

In Hastings, Christmas 1944 turned out to be the sunniest since records began and with crowds thronging the seafront there was an almost pre-war atmosphere. The Ministry of Food granted every ration book holder extra rations; 8 ounces of sugar and margarine and 8 ounces of sweets for children. The meat allocation rose from 1/2d to 1/10d worth but all this was available once only, between 10th December and 6th January. Along with a dwindling supply of utilitarian goods, National Savings Certificates were promoted as a patriotic and desirable gift.

1945

With the arrival of 1945, Hastings and St Leonards began to look to its post-war future and the more practical members of the business community realised that the quickest way to recovery was to restore and exploit the assets the town already owned, its holiday accommodation and attractions. In an article in the Drapers Record, Mr Clifford, the local chairman of the Defence Areas Hotel and Catering Industry Survival Movement wrote; 'The banned area seaside hotels would need vast supplies to make them ready to receive guests'. For the affected towns he quoted figures in millions of items needed; carpets curtains, blankets, bed and table linen and towels. This was above and beyond the costs of repairs, refurnishing and providing supplies of catering equipment. The Hastings Corporation unveiled its first holiday promotion poster since 1939, captioned; 'Hastings is getting ready for your invasion', a curious choice of words in the circumstances. At intervals during this period, public air raid sirens were still being tested.

Dear Hannah,

Our first fall of snow at Wood End, just after Christmas, turned the garden into a magical landscape, the steep, snow-covered rockeries and conifer shrubberies took on an Alpine appearance and Logs Hill became a sledge-run. The sitting room of our new home was very cosy, compensating for the chill of the rough-stone-floored kitchen and the dangerously temperamental hot water geyser over the bath. My awareness of a war going on slipped away, as I spent my free time reading, writing or listening to the radio or playing outside, while my father prepared the gardens for the new season. His employer's war service was firstly as a RAF Flight Lieutenant, in administration and subsequently, with the American Red Cross. I never understood what that meant, apart from him wearing a smart uniform of excellent quality and his being a source of provisions unobtainable to others. Via him, my mother came into possession of a supply of soft, khaki American Army blankets. One of these she dyed dark green and turned into a coat for me. (I suffered much teasing at school about this). Supplies of good things to eat put in an appearance in our house; American tinned fruit, meat, cheese, butter and occasionally, French glace fruits. And piles of American magazines, 'Time' and 'Life' and from these I gathered my first impressions of that free and wealthy nation. Pages full of pictures of beautiful, happy girls and handsome men and mouth-watering food adverts!

We were more fortunate than some; we had come through the war with the family unharmed, we had a roof over our head and my parents were in a steady job. It was not so for many. At the end of February 1945, some wartime statistics were published; since the war began, 307,201 members of the Empire's armed forces had been killed in action and 60, 585 British civilians by enemy bombs. Along with this went massive destruction of the country's housing stock. If every family were to have a home of their own, the country would need 750,000 new dwellings to meet the demand. The government planned to give priority release from the forces to hundreds of thousands of building workers.

It came as quite a blow to me in my contented little world to learn that Ron, in spite of his earlier serious illness, was to be considered for military service. At the time he was undergoing training in a company at Croydon that made surgical instruments and I expected to be able to enjoy his company at home for some time.

With Very Much Love, Gran'ma.

In Hastings, during the run up to Easter, workmen set about repairing sea-battered beach groynes, a sight so unusual that crowds gathered to watch. The re-opening of Hastings Pier was considered but it was decided this was out of the question, for at least one, if not two years. As the pier was not de-requisitioned, a small government rent was still being paid for it. There was also a severe shortage of labour and building materials, so houses, hotels and guesthouses had priority. The Food Control Committee wrestled with the problems arising from the expected influx of holiday visitors, mainly the granting of licenses to catering establishments and the shortage of staff to run them. Easter brought 2,000 rail arrivals, as well as coach trippers. Bomb-scarred Hastings did its best to re-create the spirit of peacetime Bank Holidays. The Queens Hotel offered a three-course meal for 3/6d and promised a good selection of pre-war wines and cigars. (From whence, I wonder)? There was an Easter dance at the Yelton Hotel, from 8.00pm to 11.45pm, tickets 5/- (25p); Billy Ballard's Hotshots Swingtet

and Now-

HASTINGS
AND
ST. LEONARDS
are getting ready for your
Invasion

A first post-war, holiday poster.
Source: Hastings in the Front Line.

provided the music. The White Rock Medicinal Baths had re-opened and for 4/- (20p) rheumatism sufferers could once again have the benefit of hot seaweed baths, (Fresh seaweed for every bath).

By mid-April, Hastings was already laying plans for victory celebrations. To further the recovery of the town, the bus service was to be improved, with a Sunday skeleton service and a later evening timetable, in the hopes of helping businesses to attract the much needed staff back to the catering and service industries. A General Election was in the offing and the town's Conservative MP, Hely Hutchinson, stepped down in favour of the party's new candidate, ex-Irish Guardsman, Major Neil Cooper-Key. The Sussex coast seemed like a Mediterranean shore that month, with temperatures of 70 degrees in the shade and the beaches full of sunbathers and swimmers. Householders were reminded that war was not yet over, with the warning that the five-mile coastal dim-out regulation had to remain in force, to avoid giving assistance to enemy submarines or other craft.

On 30th April came the news of Hitler's suicide. After a hasty marriage ceremony in a Berlin bunker, to his mistress, Eva Braun, she took poison and Hitler shot himself. The bodies were placed in a shell hole and set alight. The Germans surrendered on Luneberg Heath on May 4th, as Montgomery read out the capitulation terms. The end of hostilities came at 3.00pm on Monday, 8th May, in an announcement from 10 Downing Street, given by Winston Churchill: 'The German war is at an end! Advance Britannia! Long live the cause of freedom! God Save the King!' A two-day public holiday was declared. The whole country immediately erupted with a spontaneous outburst of rejoicing. The local paper said: 'Hastings and St Leonards celebrated with mingled joy and thankfulness but with thoughts of those still engaged in war in the Far East'. At the Fishmarket, a huge crowd of people of all ages were gathered under a canopy of flags and bunting and the fishing boats were decked with flags. There was street dancing and singing and a large bonfire was lit on the Rock-A-Nore beach and thunder flashes were let off. Joyce Brewer said of that time: "Oh, what a lovely day it was! My family went down to the Old Town to join in victory celebrations but I had to continue delivering milk so I couldn't join them. My sister told me that it was a wonderful feeling to be among a huge crowd of happy people. We could now look forward to having no more bombs, planes, doodlebugs or blacked out streets and homes and no more fears. We could live normal lives and catch up on all we had missed during those six years of war". People organised victory street parties, dragging their tables and chairs into the road and in spite of rationing, conjured up party food for the children.

Monica heard the news of the end of the war from her farm worker friend: "She came rushing into the cowshed, where I was standing, high up, whitewashing the rafters. She shouted, "It's all over, the war's over!" Everywhere there was a sense of relief and people tried to arrange parties, wherever possible". On VE Day, Irish Guardsman Ivor White was among the huge crowd that was encroaching on Winston

VE Day street party, Cranbrook Road, Hastings. Frank Strudwick in right foreground, seated.
Source: Unknown

Churchill's open car, in the City of London's Parliament Square. He said: "Someone did me a big favour when they pushed me onto the running board of the great man's slowly moving vehicle. I stretched out my hand towards Winnie, and shouted the Irish

Ivor White (circled) in London's VE Day crowds. Source: Press

Guards famous battle cry, 'Up the Mick's!" Grasping my hand momentarily, Winston replied, "Well done, The Mick's" and a few, brief seconds of history were to remain in my memory for a lifetime". The following Sunday, 10,000 Hastings and St Leonards people gathered at Alexandra Park for a thanksgiving service. The Hastings Mayor took the salute, as a mile-long victory parade, numbering 3,000-3,500, representing almost every form of war and home front services, marched past the War Memorial and into the park.

Dear Hannah,

When I heard the news on the 8th May, I felt the surge of joy experienced by almost everyone at the time. At my begging, my mother hunted out a scrap of red, white and blue ribbon for my hair and I put on a white dress that had red and blue spots and felt in harmony with the patriotic mood. That part of Chislehurst was too refined for street parties but I listened to the victory broadcasts on the radio, then I danced round the gardens, which were full of spring blossoms and scents. All these years later, one sniff at bluebells and for me, it's VE day again!

While I was researching for this book, I saw the picture of the VE Day celebrations in the Hastings local paper and my eyes pricked with tears. It really was that kind of tremendous event for all of us who were there. I read through the reports of Hastings street parties and a name sprang out at me. A Mr Fryatt, of 54, Belmont Road, (close to the Old

153

Town) had been instrumental in organising the street's victory party for the children. I bet that was RAF man John Bryant's Mr Fryatt, who provided the potluck supper after church; what a hospitable man!

Within less than two weeks, the realities of victory began to bite on the home front. Rations of bacon, cooking fat and soap were cut; supplies were to be shared with the liberated European countries. The British weekly cooking fat ration went from two to one ounce per person, per week; bacon from four to three and the soap ration was cut by an eighth. For your 21st century arithmetic, one ounce is 28.3 grammes. Demobilisation of British servicemen began in mid-June, starting with 30,000 per week, to rise to 60,000 by August. Each was kitted out with a set of clothing, including a three piece suit that was popularly called, 'the demob suit'.

I was sometimes allowed to go alone on the bus to Bromley, to visit the cinema. I think one of the films I saw in 1945 was 'Just William' and I enjoyed it so much I decided to see it round again, you could in those days. This meant sitting through the newsreel and on this day its content was appalling. It was footage of the liberating of a concentration camp; I do not know which one. These days, almost everyone is familiar with these tragic and shocking images but as I sat there alone, in the darkness, the pictures were burned into my memory. This may sound trivial but even today I dislike fabric with broad stripes, to me this beastly concentration camp uniform became the symbol of the suffering of the victims. I arrived home upset and my parent's were angry but there was no censorship on newsreels and the film had been 'U' certificate. Victory euphoria soon evaporated.

With Very much Love Gran'ma

In the week leading up to the Whitsun Bank Holiday, five British minesweepers were seen off Hastings, combing the Channel for stray mines and making ready for when merchant vessels and pleasure steamers could plot their own courses, without directions from a convoy. It turned out to be a very a lively holiday for the town, with a total of 20,000 visitors. That same week, a secret about Hastings' wartime defences was disclosed. If the Germans had invaded, a sheet of flame would have burst up from the sea. Oil was to have been conveyed out to sea, via pipes, from big, camouflaged reservoirs, one at White Rock, one at the Fishmarket and two at Rock-A-Nore. The oil would have been ignited by chemical means, on contact with water. The reservoirs resembled the military Martello Towers, which were constructed when Napoleon threatened these same shores. The purpose of the reservoirs remained a mystery to many local people, until this post-war disclosure. The General Election followed in early July and there was a good voter turnout. There was a three-week delay before the final result because the service personnel postal votes had to be gathered; the Conservatives were victorious, with a final count of 27,177 from a total of vote of 36,181. In the middle of July, Hastings roads returned to full lighting with the switching on of 3,000 street lamps.

Hastings man, Norman Redford was far from home during the victory celebrations and playing a peripheral role in a dramatic moment of history. He said: "On the 24th May 1945 I was stationed in Luneberg, Germany, at the 2nd Army Headquarters, Defence Company's Transport Section. I was a driver from the 2nd Battalion Monmouthshire Regiment and on this particular day I was a duty driver and one of my tasks was to take meals to all the Guard Posts in and around the Headquarters. A friend of mine, Lance Corporal Bill Carrot, was on guard duty at No.31a, Uelzener Strasse, in Luneburg. When I arrived there, I sensed that something strange was going on, as there were lots of high-ranking officers and military police in evidence. I was eventually able ask Bill what was happening. He said, 'Come back later and bring your camera' (Among the other odd jobs, I was asked to do was to act as the unofficial, army photographer).

A couple of hours later, I went back to No.31a, where Bill was on the lookout for me and he told me to go round the back, where there was an open window. I scrambled over the windowsill and got into a room. Lying on the floor was a body, which I immediately recognised as that of Heinrich Himmler. The body was not in a very good position for taking a photograph, so we propped it against an upturned table, which we had covered with a blanket. I then took the photograph and I left the room as quickly as I could. That night I developed the film, using a small portable developing tank and the next day I took the negatives to the local chemist, to get some prints and enlargements, which cost

1945

Heinrich Himmler

me a few bars of chocolate and some cigarettes. I gave one copy to Bill, and one to the duty officer, in charge of the guard. This was probably a mistake because he immediately demanded the negative for H.Q., saying that I would be breaking the official secrets act if I kept the negative or spoke to anyone about what I had done. Luckily, I had already had many copies made. Eventually, I think that half of the 2nd Army HQ personnel acquired a copy of the photograph. Years later, in March 1985, Bill Carrot's son found this picture of Himmler in his father's wardrobe and sent it to The Daily Mirror. They printed the story on their front page on Monday May 6th 1985, almost 40 years after I took the photo. I contacted the Mirror, telling them that it was me who had taken the picture, and they got in touch with Bill's local TV station in Norwich. A few days later I met Bill for the first time since we were demobbed in January 1946. We appeared together on television to recall our part in the demise of Heinrich Himmler".

At the time of his death, Himmler was naked, as he was being searched to see if he had the means of suicide. He had secreted a cyanide capsule in his mouth, which he bit into. His captors tried desperately to rinse out his mouth, to no avail. For the purposes of the photograph, Himmler was hastily dressed in a British army shirt and a blanket was thrown over the lower part of his body; his spectacles were lost, so those in the picture were not his but a borrowed pair. Heinrich Himmler was the son of a devout Catholic schoolmaster and began his working life as a chicken

Himmler's corpse. Source: Norman Redford.

156

1945

farmer. He was drawn to the Nazi Party in the early 1920s, where he quickly rose through the ranks. He became the second most powerful figure of the Nazi regime, after Hitler and was the architect of the country's police state and the founder of the SS, Germany's elite fighting force. Himmler also presided over the highly organized system of Nazi concentration and death camps, which exterminated 11 million people, including millions of Jews, as well as other sections of society the regime considered to be 'unnecessary', as well as those who dared to oppose Hitler. Himmler's body, along with a rough, wooden cross, was buried in an unmarked, woodland grave.

Dear Hannah,

Norman Redford went to become one of Hastings best known commercial photographers, many local people will recognise his name. I have carried this story into Europe, partly to follow locals through war service and also because of your own European connections. Politicians are currently exercising themselves over the problems of trying to turn Europe into one entity, while its peoples continue to serve this end as they have done for centuries, by falling in love with those from different parts of the continent! As a result of this phenomenon, you have Dutch, Belgian and Italian as well as English relatives. This story of your family in WWII would not be complete without some mention of them. British people acknowledge that terrible though the war was for us, at least we did not suffer our country being occupied by the enemy, as did much of Europe.

Your Dutch and Belgian great-grandparents died some years ago and your Hastings-dwelling, 'continental' grandmother, much younger than I am, has only a few fragments of WWII family history to tell. She knows that your Dutch great-grandmother was in the Resistance and was awarded a medal for her courage after the war. Your Belgian great-grandmother was a seamstress and when the Germans caught her stealing potatoes

Hannah's Belgian great-grandparents
in post-war times.

157

from a field she was spared the usual punishment of transportation,
usually meted out for this offence and was put to work in a garment
factory, making army uniform hats. Her husband was compelled to be
a driver for the Germans and was fortunate in being treated quite well.

The grandmother of your half-Italian cousins was not able tell her
wartime story, so a contemporary, Espero, drew this picture of the life
of his wartime childhood in Milan, on her behalf. I found his
recollections very moving. It is due to his being one of your Aunt
Barbara's adult language students, in her Milan-based School of
English, that we have his story. Until he wrote this account of
childhood, his Italian children and grandchildren had had no idea of
what he had endured and seen during the war.

With Very much Love, Gran'ma

Espero said: "To describe how a child experiences war only has
meaning if it is compared with how life was before. My parents earned
their living selling fruit and vegetables, on a stall in Saint Stephen
market in Milan and for us it was quite a comfortable life. I had two
sisters, Daniela was sixteen years old, Lidia was nine and I was six.
The care of her younger siblings was left to Daniela and she didn't give
much attention to the task, so we had plenty of time to enjoy freedom
with our friends. In the mornings we went to school, with enough
pocket money to buy the mid morning breakfast of chocolate and fresh
bread rolls. Sometime we saved the money for the roll so that we could
give ourselves a treat, by buying a piece of nut cake, just outside
school. After lunch, with my homework done, I was free to play
football in a field near my house or we used to jump on the back of a
horse-driven carriage, at that time the most popular way of transport. I
loved those happy days.

Then the war came and all the city's squares become filled with
excited people, loudspeakers were set up, and Mussolini, 'Il Duce',
made his speech. He announced the beginning of hostilities, a word I
did not understand. I thought nothing would change for me. Then
disaster struck, my father left us, which reduced us to poverty. The war
began with the presence of an isolated enemy aircraft, which dropped
a bomb on a house nearby; there were no causalities, just damage. This

event changed my idea of war as being a matter of battles between soldiers in trenches. At first, the bombing of cities was occasional but with time, it became more frequent and brought me the most terrifying experience of my life.

One evening, I went to the cinema with my mother and as we were coming out, the alarm warned of an air raid. We tried to get home quickly but when we were halfway there, the bombardment started, attacking the main hospital and the warden advised mum to take cover in an air raid shelter. We refused and made our way through Saint Stephen Square, while the bombardment was at its peak; reaching our home made us feel safe. We lay down on our stomachs on the bedroom floor and, looking through the window, we watched a terrifying but at the same time, fascinating spectacle. The night sky was illuminated with 'Bengalis', shining candles, dropped by aircraft, to light up their targets. There were white lines in the sky from the machine gun bullets, anti-aircraft shells were being shot from our air defences and there were tremendous explosions, made by bombs dropped from the planes. Very soon our fear overcame us, so we joined the neighbours, who had already gathered beneath some the steps, under the delusion that these would have provided protection. Here it was pitch dark, nothing could be seen and the noise of exploding bombs was overwhelming. I jumped with fear at each one. I realized that what I should fear most weren't the explosions but the whizzing sound of the falling bombs, more terrible and frightening because it lasted longer. My fear made me wet my trousers repeatedly. Somebody started praying and the others joined in. A strange thought came to my mind; people in every shelter were certainly praying but bombs had already been dropped and were still falling, whom would God favour, I wondered? I just begged the torment would end. That was the cruellest bombardment for Milan, when it was over we came out into the open and saw complete desolation around us. The hospital and other buildings were demolished, few structures survived, some of those remaining were burning. Among the rubble, people were already digging, trying to rescue survivors or useful belongings. I now understood the real meaning of war and even today, this is my most powerful memory.

For family reasons and because of the increasing number of air raids, my family was scattered and I was sent to a little college near Bolzano, in the north east of Italy, in the Dolomites. Lidia was sent to Bergamo, north of Milan, while Daniela and my mum remained in the city. Soon the war faded from my life, the only reminder of it was food rationing and the severe discipline of the boarding school, which was home to three hundreds boys, from six to twelve years old. The school was of a military type and its regime of study, punishments and play became my life and family was forgotten. The most miserable period was bedtime, announced by trumpet. The darkness left me with time for myself. My mind, free from the activities of the day, dwelt on memories, dreams about the future but mostly on the lack of affection. During September 1943, Italy capitulated to the Allies and suddenly, the enemy became a friend and the friend became an enemy, as the Germans became an occupying force, supported by the Italian fascists. Our boarding school had to move from Bolzano. Territorially speaking, since The Great War, the residents had been Italians but in fact, by their culture and traditions, they were Austrian. We moved to a town 20 miles from Milan and so fell back into the war. Germans and Fascists controlled the area but the partisans, who were hiding in the mountains, were conducting guerrilla warfare. After each partisan attack on the enemy, reprisals were taken on the population. For each German soldier killed, ten local people were picked from the inhabitants and executed. In Milan, my sister Daniela was caught in a Gestapo search, when she was discovered visiting the home of a Jewish family. She and the family were sent to Germany, to a 'working field'. Only my sister came back.

The planes of our former enemies, now our allies, continued to bomb but in a more precise manner. Not on houses any more but on railway stations, soldiers' billets, main roads and bridges. One day, there was an air attack on a bridge, only three kilometres away from us. I clearly saw the plane, carrying two bombs under its wings. I saw it dive and drop the bombs on the bridge and it was very distressing for me, as it revived my earlier terror. It was only later on, during the evening, when I heard music coming from a nearby bar that the sensation lifted and I felt a moment of peace. I'll never forget that song and even now, when I hear it, I re-experience my feelings of that time.

We lived in a waking nightmare. Italians were divided into two fighting parties and in the middle were the people of our village, waiting impatiently for the Americans to arrive and bring the war to an end. Many people were listening in secret to the BBC broadcasts. This was strictly forbidden and could be punished by death. The station was called Radio Londra and we believed it was giving the true news on the war and we knew it differed enormously from that of the regime. Being reported to the police at that time, even falsely, could have cost your life but that sort of risk was part of normal, daily life. Time seemed to move so slowly. My mother would come to see me, when she could, on her bicycle. She always brought me something for me to eat and she stood and watched me, while I eagerly ate it. I offered to share part of it with her but she always refused, pretending not to be hungry but I knew it was a lie. Finally the Americans arrived they gave us chocolate, cigarettes, chewing gum and lots of smiles. Liberation brought a feeling of great joy; people were singing and dancing in streets and courtyards.

Days of retribution followed, as people took their revenge against the Fascists and their supporters. Not a day passed without executions. The heads of Fascist women were shaved and they were paraded barefoot through the streets, as the populace hurled every kind of insult at them. At this time too, a report to the police could have cost your life. One day, in Milan's Loreto Square, in the same spot where Fascist atrocities had taken place, the corpses of Mussolini, his lover and several of his supporters, were hung upside down. Some were brought to the square already dead, others were killed there. I was there and I saw these things. Slowly, we got back to normal life, many families were reunited but others were not. The war was gone and with it went my youth".

Espero with his mother and sister.

Ivor White was sent to join the occupying forces in Germany and sailed out from Dover on HMS Princess Astrid, in late September. The ship was a Royal Navy-operated Landing Craft Carrier and one of a fleet of former Belgian cross-channel passenger ships, which were requisitioned for war service. HMS Princess Astrid took part in many wartime excursions, including the Dieppe commando raids and the D-Day landings. Ivor spoke about his crossing: "In the Channel there were still mines floating about, which had broken loose from their moorings and had been missed by the navy minesweepers. There was a moon, and the sea was quite choppy and I remember spending most of the journey on deck, up at the sharp end of this old cross-channel ferry, commandeered to serve as a troop ship. Mounted on the forward deck was a powerful searchlight, which was continually scanning the water ahead, for any signs of a mine, as we slowly made our way towards Calais. A journey that takes 75 minutes today must have lasted more than four hours that night. Fresh from the rigours of training with the Irish Guards, in the Welsh mountains, under live fire, to make us keep our heads down, we heard the comforting words of our Sergeant Major, that we were, 'all in the same boat'! I suppose the threat of hitting the odd mine didn't cause too much fear amongst us; looking back it seems scarier now than it actually was at the time.

We landed safely in Calais docks, to be herded onto a train that had wooden seats and had obviously been used by the Germans for transporting prisoners. My knowledge of the language was sufficient to read some of the graffiti scrawled on the carriages and the warnings in German not to look out of the windows. It was very dark, as the train slowly made its way to the ruins of Krefeld, the first town on the German border, where there was a very large military transit camp. Thousands of troops, of all the allied nations passed through this camp near the Dutch border, many of them going home for the first time since the end of the fighting. Here, quite by chance, I met a Canadian soldier, who had been stationed in Battle Abbey and had been taken prisoner in Normandy. I recognised his cap badge, but I have no idea now what regiment he was in but he was part of the 8th Canadian Reconnoitre Battalion. We spent the rest of the night and the next day at Krefeld, de-lousing and waiting for another train".

Ivor's arrival in Germany was three months after the war was over. Of this time he said: "We found the city of Cologne in ruins, as the result of the RAF 1,000 bomber raids. The only useable bridge across the

1945

Rhine was a pontoon, a floating platform, which swayed as we drove over. Cologne Cathedral seemed to have escaped the destruction and towered above the ruined city. There had been a few feeble attempts by old ladies and children to rescue some of their belongings from the rubble, where hundreds of dead bodies were still buried. There was a distinct smell associated with all this devastation that reminded me of the bombed sites I saw in London after our Blitz. The sight of slightly bedraggled and very polite children following us around, waiting for the discarded butt-end from a cigarette, soon parted us from our NAAFI rations. Chocolate, cigarettes and tins of corned beef were sometimes traded for souvenirs on the Black Market, but quite often were just given to children, those whose fathers had either not come home or were in some displaced persons camp, waiting to be identified. I was soon to experience my first Christmas in Germany, in the picturesque and almost undamaged little town of Gummersbach, in the Rhineland, where the 2nd Battalion Irish Guards were to stay for a few months.

I 'volunteered' to become an officer's servant, known as a batman in other regiments. I was privileged to live in the commandeered, private house of a local factory owner. It was here that I began to learn German, which came in handy when negotiating 'deals' with the local residents. For a few cigarettes I could get my laundry done, films developed and printed, and alterations and repairs done to my own and my officer's uniforms. Among other duties, I was occasionally assigned to the Hamburg Law Courts, as a courtroom sentry during trials for various cases, from those of the major war criminals to the petty offence of stealing coal. My growing knowledge of the German language came in handy here, and I was able to compare my progress with the official interpreter's account of the proceedings.

I made many friends while serving in post-war Hamburg. One, who was just a child in 1945, used to call at the barracks each day to get a bowl of soup from a field kitchen, which we set up outside the barrack gates. She carried her young brother in her arms, so that they would be allowed two helpings. Then they would go home to share the soup with their Mum. In 1999, this former, hungry child saw an article about my Irish Guards website in the German newspaper "Hamburger Abendblatt" and she contacted me and has been writing to me ever since".

1945

The 1945 August Bank Holiday Weekend brought 40,000 visitors to Hastings and St Leonards and because of lack of accommodation, some slept in the suntrap shelters on the seafront. Due to staff shortages, there were long queues for cafes, restaurants and ice cream shops. It was reckoned at the time that hotel and guesthouse residents spent on an average of eight pounds per person per week and day-trippers a pound each. The beaches were packed and scores of the small, on-hire catamarans dotted the sea. Six ratings and two officers from the sloop, HMS Hastings, adopted by the town after Warship Week, came as the guests of their sponsors. Shortages of all kinds of goods still existed and 'Vigilant' had something to say about this, with reference to cigarettes and alcohol: 'It is a disgrace that there are visitors who come to Hastings and St Leonards for the sole the purpose of going from shop to shop, until all the tobacconists and licensed premises are sold out'.

On the 6th and 9th of August, the dropping of atom bombs on Hiroshima and Nagasaki brought about the end of the war with Japan. These two cities were almost totally destroyed, with immense loss of life and horrendous injuries. Japan surrendered on the 14th August and the Allied Forces were ordered to suspend hostilities immediately. Hastings local newspaper reported the town's response to the victory over Japan by saying, 'There were not the immediate scenes of public demonstration that there had been at the announcement of the ending of the war in Europe. Many people were at work when the news came through'. Never the less, another round of street parties, singing and dancing, bonfires, thunder flashes and wild behaviour ensued on the following official two-day holiday. A soldier was seen standing on the platform of a Hastings bus, playing the bagpipes, regardless of the boarding and alighting passengers and the Queen Victoria statue in Warrior Square was decorated with a beach sign that declared, 'Bathing Now Prohibited.'

1945

Dear Hannah,

Of course, I remember the end of the war in the Far East but the implications of the dropping of the atom bomb were lost on a child and quite a few adults too. These days I get emails from American children, who are doing a project on WWII and they mostly ask me what I had thought at the time about Pearl Harbour, Hiroshima and Nagasaki. They seem almost unaware that the war that took place in Europe was such a massive conflict. By August 1945 I had joined a Methodist Church youth group, so for the Victory over Japan celebrations I did have the experience of going to a party, in the street where the church stood. It was fun; just having tables and chairs set in the road was enough to make it special, add party games, music, flags, free sandwiches and lemonade and it was a huge treat! By the way, I was not a Methodist as such. Following my early upbringing in the High Anglican Church, as soon as I was able to go to church by myself, I tried various denominations. It certainly taught me to be very accepting of other forms of religious worship.

The first summer in our new home passed pleasantly for me. The boss and his family went away quite often and left my parents in charge, which gave us an opportunity to enjoy a bit more high living. What better way was there to take care of a lovely house other than to occupy it? We did no harm and it pleased me to once again enjoy some spacious, well-furnished rooms and to delve into the book collection of the employer's daughter, who was three years older than me. I particularly remember her copy of the book, Ballet Shoes, by Noel Streatfield. After peeping in the boss' wardrobe, my brother Ron took the opportunity for another 'fancy dress' session. He looked splendid to me as a RAF Lieutenant, an American Red Cross officer and, as the family were Mc-something, there was full highland dress to complete the costume parade.

Perhaps you are slightly shocked, Hannah, at us occupying the master's house, rather similar to the weasels in Wind in the Willows. At one time my family would never have considered doing such a thing but the war had changed so much. It had emboldened people to behave out of character and take a different view of property and status. War is a great social leveller and the deference once automatically due to

165

those my father wryly called the 'aristocrinocracy' was disappearing. We had never been forelock-tuggers anyhow and the war had made experienced, live-in domestic staff very hard to come by. Perhaps we were the new 'aristocrinocracy!'

With Very Much Love From Gran'ma.

In early September, at Hastings Town Hall, there was an official stand down of the Civil Defence workers of the WVS. In her address, the Regional Administrator, Lady Worsley spoke of the wartime work of the WVS being a fine job, well done and she praised the unselfish service and courage of the volunteers through the past six years.

The end of the war brought Monica the fulfilment of a dream: "The farm where I worked in Westfield was sold in October 1945 and I was sorry to be leaving but as I was 17 years old, the Women's Land Army would accept me. I was delighted when I became a member, after an initial interview in Lewes and a medical in Hastings. My uniform soon followed, three enormous parcels, I had never had so many new clothes at once and all were of good quality. I thought I was having all my birthdays and Christmases rolled into one".

The December 1st edition of the Hastings Observer published the story of the re-naming of the pub next door to the town Hall. Previously called The Central Hotel, it was to be called The GI, as a tribute to the American forces and their friendly associations with the British people. Sergeant William Hastings, of Fort Worth, Texas, aged 25 and recently married to Joyce Hopwood, an English girl, was chosen for the duty of unveiling the newly painted sign, which depicted a smiling GI. The Hastings Mayor and a number of local dignitaries were present, as well as American Army visitors, some of whom were also taking back English brides to the United States. The newspaper article said that Sergeant Hastings was presented with an engraved silver tankard, engraved with the pub sign but he says he never actually

Joyce and Sgt W. Hastings on their wedding day.

received it. What he did get was a postcard-sized reproduction of the original pub sign, which was painted by Violet Rutter, from life sketches, supplied by the American authorities. William Hastings carried this picture in his wallet for years, hoping he would eventually find someone who could tell him more about the pub. It was his approach to a Hastings website in 2000 that brought the story to light once more. In 2001, his children commissioned an American artist to make a copy of the pub sign and it now hangs in the ex-sergeant's home, as a memento of a unique event.

Sgt Hastings' pub sign postcard

In December, to the benefit of future historians, ex-Major J Manwaring Baines took up the post of Curator of Hastings Museum, where he would spend the rest of his working life. While serving with the army in Scotland, Manwaring Baines had an accident that kept him in hospital for a prolonged period. It was during this enforced break from duty that the idea germinated in his mind for his book 'Historic Hastings', which has become the 'bible' for local researchers. 'Vigilant' viewed the coming festivities as a salvage opportunity, informing his readers that, 'if each family in the country put out an extra half pound of clean, waste paper it would make 40 million sugar cartons or 12 million sheets of plasterboard, enough to put ceilings on 12,000 homes'. However, the prospects of there being much extra paper in households were doubtful; festive decorations, crackers and wrapping paper were practically unobtainable, as were the Christmas gifts to wrap.

A Captain Cheek and his wife offered their home, in Palace Chambers on Hastings seafront, as Christmas honeymoon accommodation to two pairs of newlyweds. Twelve months before the bridegrooms had been prisoners of war in Japan but in 1945 they spent the holiday in gracious rooms, overlooking broad views of the English Channel, enjoying breakfast in bed and all the seasonal hospitality the town could offer.

Dear Hannah,

Ron passed his medical and was accepted into the Royal Air Force. He went in under the wartime scheme, called Duration of Present Emergencies, which still existed, even though peace had been declared. I was so anxious about him and my feelings became so raw that after a mild ticking off at school, I burst into tears and could not be consoled. I feared my brother was not tough enough to survive service life (how wrong I was, he says it was the making of him). He went away on 5th December and was back on leave for Christmas; maybe it wouldn't be so bad after all. Derrick came out of the navy and was obliged to live under his father's roof, a situation that was not agreeable to an independent young man who had spent four years fighting at sea and there was tension in the house. That Christmas was the last one we were to spend as a complete family for some years.

Ron Burkin, to whom this book is dedicated.

As 1945 drew to a close, there was one more 'enemy' for my ex-Home Guard father to encounter. Like all his comrades, he was stood down in October. The HG storekeeping was badly organised and hardly anyone handed back every item; my father still wore parts of his Home Guard uniform as work gear. The only things they were strict about being returned were rifles, which were numbered, and the ten rounds of ammunition given to each man.

I was still a regular attendee at the Methodist Church youth club and was taking part in evening rehearsals for their New Year pantomime, Cinderella. I was very accustomed to walking home alone in the dark and never afraid. One night, quite close to my house, a man on a bike accosted me, grabbed my clothes, drew me close to his face and spoke about things a child should not hear. I beat him off and ran into our garden, where my father found me, crying. On hearing what had happened, he got on his bike and, armed with the Home Guard bayonet he had never returned to the stores, he set off in search of the man. From my adult viewpoint I am grateful that my father did not find him but at the time, as a result of a childhood influenced by a background of war and killing, my law-abiding father's aggressive response did not seem particularly remarkable to me.

In April 1948, my parent's employer bought a house and farm at Fairlight, just outside Hastings and my family moved into the worker's bungalow in Peter James Lane. This, my, dear little Hannah, is how it chanced that you were born in the town associated with the most famous battle in British history. As you grow up, the story of how my generation of children and young people lived through a 20th century war will also be just history.

I hope that this account and these letters will bring you closer to understanding those momentous times.

With very much love to you, my dear grandchild, from Victoria, your 'Story Gran'ma'

1945